AQA Primary Assessing
Assessing Reading
Teacher's Handbook

Janet Mort

Text © Janet Mort 2008
Original illustrations © Nelson Thornes Ltd 2008

The right of Janet Mort to be identified as author of this work has been asserted by her in accordance with the Copyright, Designs and Patents Act 1988.

All rights reserved. No part of this publication may be reproduced or transmitted in any form or by any means, electronic or mechanical, including photocopy, recording or any information storage and retrieval system, without permission in writing from the publisher or under licence from the Copyright Licensing Agency Limited, of Saffron House, 6-10 Kirby Street, London EC1N 8TS.

Any person who commits any unauthorised act in relation to this publication may be liable to criminal prosecution and civil claims for damages.

Published in 2008 by:
Nelson Thornes Ltd
Delta Place
27 Bath Road
CHELTENHAM
GL53 7TH
United Kingdom

08 09 10 11 12 / 10 9 8 7 6 5 4 3 2 1

A catalogue record for this book is available from the British Library

978-0-7487-9994-7

Illustrations by Paul Gamble

Cover photograph courtesy of BananaStock Ltd

Page make-up by Fakenham Photosetting Ltd

Printed in Croatia by Zrinski

Contents

What do we mean by Assessment?	4
Understanding how Assessment works	8
Using Assessment to help children learn	11
Using progress targets to move children from level to level	19
Assessment of reading in practice	25
Helping children to formulate their own questions	30
Helping children read & respond to poetry	32
Dealing with common problems in children's reading	37
Preparing for SATs	50
Photocopy masters	56
Glossary of terms	75
Assessment game: A day in Pompeii	76

Assessment is the process by which we as teachers – and our children as learners – make judgements on their work in order to gauge progress. It enables learners to understand and feel confident about what they can do, and highlights the skills they need to consolidate and develop in order to make progress. Accurate and systematic assessment not only heightens learners' awareness of their strengths and weaknesses, but also informs our lesson planning. In addition, the formal grading or 'levelling' of written outcomes guides us in structuring our teaching groups and in determining the nature and levels of support that children require.

What do we mean by Assessment?

The form of assessment with which parents are probably most familiar is the End of Key Stage Assessments (**EKSAs**, commonly known as SATs). Much has been said and written about the extent to which SATs effectively 'measure' the quality of schools (and 'rank' them), and the extent to which they are valuable in genuinely raising educational standards.

At the same time, other ways of assessing pupils' progress are being trialled and introduced. The most significant of these are the **Single Level Tests**, external tests closely linked to teacher assessment. Using evidence gathered in the classroom, teachers make judgements about a child's reading level using the **criteria** on the **Assessing Pupil Progress (APP)** guidelines. Teachers then enter children for that particular reading level at one of two points in the academic year. **External marking** of the paper then either confirms teacher judgements, or the child is not awarded the particular level for which he or she has been entered.

Although these alternative arrangements for Key Stage 2 assessment are in their early stages, the implications for us as classroom teachers are clear.

Increasingly the focus is on assessment as part of day-to-day work. Teachers will become much more familiar with **Assessment Focuses** in literacy and use them in a more focused way to make judgements on children's reading and writing. Teachers will also have a better understanding of a child's individual profile in reading and writing.

Finally, using externally marked tests to support individual teachers' judgements will mean that judgements can be validated. For many, APP and the Single Level Tests combine both formative and summative assessments in a way which helps teachers and enables children to make better progress.

Concern is often expressed that many teachers adopt a superficial, short-term approach to the SATs and 'teach to the test'. Learning in English is achieved in the long term not the short term and involves revisiting work already covered again and again. If we do not consolidate 'progress' achieved by 'hot-housing' methods we often find that children cannot apply what they have learned in different contexts. Development in English is not necessarily linear. Children may demonstrate unexpected skills despite not having fully grasped apparently easier aspects of work; assessment helps the teacher to recognise such anomalies.

Most importantly, we should be careful not to reduce assessment in English to a set of hierarchical skills. Language use is creative, and there would not be much great literature if writing could be produced to a formula. In reading, there will always be a tension between 'right answers' and interesting/valid personal responses, and in writing there will always be writers who break some of the generally accepted rules of punctuation for effect. Assessment needs to take this into account and will then reward us with a much better picture of a child's strengths, progress and potential.

Research indicates that students are better motivated to learn and make faster progress when they are actively involved in the assessment process. In recent years, it has become part of good classroom practice to share learning objectives with pupils – to shift the emphasis from the teacher to the learner – so that pupils can better understand what they are learning, why they are learning it and how activities might develop their skills. The more reflective the children become, the more responsible for their learning they are likely to feel, and the more keen they are to improve. The **Assessment for Learning** strategy now embedded in schools' practice represents a welcome shift towards student-centred learning.

Types of assessment

There are four main types of assessment:

- **Formative assessment** is the process by which a teacher observes, evaluates, discusses or marks a piece of work and identifies specific strengths and weaknesses in it in order to provide a focus for teacher/student discussion and student self-analysis/reflection.

- **Diagnostic assessment** results from formative assessment; i.e. we use the feedback to determine the pupils needs and how he/she needs to plan to meet them. Diagnostic assessment might also take the form of tests specifically developed to measure a child's particular difficulties.

- **Summative assessment** is the feedback given to a student at the end of a marked piece of work which highlights strengths and weaknesses to be addressed. It is also a term which can be used to describe more formal end-of-unit or end-of-phase tests.

- **Assessment for learning,** which might be seen as 'day-to-day' assessment, is a process which is concerned not just with outcomes, but with promoting the whole learning process. By establishing a classroom climate in which both teachers and learners are actively engaged in this process, assessment has more impact and value.

Whilst diagnostic assessment, by its very nature, will be objective, both formative and summative assessment are likely to be selective and partial, targeted to the levels of ability of and perceived priorities for the students concerned.

> 'Assessment for learning is the process of seeking and interpreting evidence for use by learners and their teachers to decide where learners are in their learning, where they need to go and how best to get there.'
>
> **Assessment Reform Group, 2002**

Just praising children's work has no formative or diagnostic value; equally, correction of every error is likely to undermine a student's self-esteem and prevent them from seeing clearly their priorities in terms of targets to work on.

Summative assessment can become formative in the sense that a folder of work gathered over a period of time might reinforce the need to revisit skills not consolidated during that time; at which point it is worth repeating that what is taught in a skills- rather than content-based subject, such as English, is not necessarily learned fully in the short term.

How does Assessment help children?

Assessment helps children improve **skills** by:

- providing them with a **context** and **purpose** for their current learning

- **reinforcing their knowledge/understanding of content and skills** (though children appreciate praise, surveys of upper KS2 children of different abilities have shown that the most important aspect of teacher feedback is the identification of what they need to improve and advice about how to do so)

- enabling them to **reflect** on their learning in order to utilise it in other contexts

- helping them to **modify their approach** to learning where appropriate

- **relaxing pressure** by providing 'time out' from 'doing'; reflection time also helps them to **consider modifications** 'on the spot' rather than allow time to lapse.

Assessment can **motivate** children by:

- heightening their **awareness of progress** made: providing encouragement whilst recognising targets for improvement

- offering them a **'teaching' role** via peer assessment; it is claimed that we remember 70% of what we explain to others.

In addition, by making teaching/learning criteria transparent, assessment can inform parents and encourage a supportive dialogue between them and their children.

How does Assessment help teachers?

Assessment **empowers** teachers by:

- helping them to **understand learners** as individuals and to recognise and understand individual/group/class strengths and weaknesses

- **monitoring rates of progress** and raising awareness of difficulties in assimilation which can help 'pinpoint' areas where support and consolidation are needed

- creating a **structured agenda for feedback** dialogues

- **informing detailed planning.**

Whilst emphasising the value of assessment in providing detailed information about skills development, a caveat is needed. A teacher's advice or suggested improvements can be counter-productive, especially when children are experimenting or responding in an original way. Sometimes learners need to be 'given their heads' to pursue their own creative approach or to exercise independent thinking. An informed personal response to reading might be more valuable than a teacher's idea of the 'right answer'. A child who is naturally able to structure ideas might be able to dispense with some stages of the planning of writing. Especially when assessing writing, teachers need to understand that English is primarily about communication and not just a set of discrete skills. Assessment should also help the teacher to appreciate individuality and to recognise that strengths and weaknesses are counterbalanced in a 'best fit' assessment.

Assessment **supports** other teachers by:

- creating a detailed profile of development which helps teachers new to the class to plan using prior knowledge
- ensuring that the new teachers have high (but realistic) expectations of children before the 'summer crop' which often necessitates reinforcement of skills previously 'learned' (learning in English being recursive, as previously stated).

How will this book help?

Many teachers find it difficult to assess children's strengths and weaknesses in reading except by using standardised tests. This book will:

- give an overview of different forms of assessment and how each helps children and teachers in the Key Stage 2 classroom
- provide a level-by-level description of children's attainment in Reading Assessment Focuses 2–6
- identify specific skills to improve children's reading
- show teachers how to find and use evidence for the assessment of reading
- provide practical ideas for teaching key reading skills
- suggest how past test papers can be used to help prepare children for tests.

In this section we look more closely at each of the main forms of assessment in terms of implications for schools and classroom practice.

Understanding how Assessment works

Formal/external assessment

APP – Assessing Pupil Progress

Currently being developed and piloted, APP supports teachers in assessing children's progress in reading through an ongoing review of their work in class. Using a relatively small number of assessment guidelines rather than long lists of assessment criteria or test marks, teachers periodically review evidence of children's reading from as broad a curriculum as possible. This gives them a profile of an individual child's particular strengths and weaknesses. When required, teachers can convert their assessments to National Curriculum levels by following a short step-by-step procedure.

Not only does it help teachers become more familiar with Assessment Focuses, it also encourages them to use a wide range of evidence of children's independent work, to make use of oral evidence and to offer children more choice of reading tasks.

APP is linked to the use of Single Level Tests, in which teachers enter children for a particular level of reading test to confirm their judgements. (See 'What do we mean by assessment?' page 4)

EKSAs (End of Key Stage Assessments)

In May each year, when Year 6 children sit EKSAs, commonly referred to as SATs, they are awarded a reading level within the range of Levels 3–5.

The test booklets always include texts of different types, usually linked by a theme. For example, in 2007 the booklet was called 'On Dangerous Ground' and contained facts about volcanoes, an account of an eruption in Pompeii and postcards and adverts about visits to modern Pompeii. Test questions cover all Assessment Focuses and vary in levels of difficulty for each text.

Children's individual levels/marks can be analysed to identify areas of strength or weakness in a schools teaching of reading in the following ways:

▶ Average boys' or girls' reading mark to compare performance by gender.

▶ Average reading mark to compare classes or cohorts.

A representative sample of papers can be selected and used to identify strengths or weaknesses of children's answers on particular Assessment Focuses.

Continuous assessment

Assessment for learning (AfL)

Assessment for learning is used increasingly in classrooms both for day-to-day assessments in reading, but also as a way of involving children in their own learning.

What do we mean by Assessment for Learning?
Assessment for Learning …

> " … is any assessment activity that informs the next steps to learning. AfL depends crucially on using the information gained.'

www.standards.dfes.gov.uk/primaryframeworks/literacy/assessment

Before the AfL approach can become part and parcel of our everyday classroom practice, we need to understand the following basic principles.

AfL is a form of **continuous assessment** which:

- can be used in a **variety of learning contexts**
- is an **integral** rather than a separate part of lessons
- can be used at **any appropriate point** in the learning process
- focuses on the **process of learning** not just the end result
- provides learners with **useful feedback** in a form which helps them recognise what they have already achieved, what they need to do to improve further and how they can achieve this improvement.

AfL enables teachers and learners to work together in an **assessment partnership** which:

- involves learners by sharing **what, why and how** they are learning

- helps both teachers and learners to **check current understanding and progress** and **make informed judgements** about what to do next
- enables children to become more reflective and independent learners through **self- and peer-assessment.**

Changing the assessment climate in YOUR classroom
If AfL is to be effective in promoting learning and raising standards, teachers need to change both ethos and classroom practice.

The classroom where AfL is not used	The AfL classroom
Ethos	
Teachers see themselves as responsible for what and how children learn	Children are involved in their own learning and are, as a result, more motivated
Teachers emphasise weaknesses to be addressed	The emphasis is on progress, achievement and constructive advice
Children see content as being most important	Children think about the whole learning process: content, skills and understanding
During the lesson	
The teacher delivers lessons without sharing purpose, process and expectations	The teacher shares these aspects of the learning process with the children
The teacher is the one who knows what the children need to do to succeed	Learners ALSO have a clear understanding of success criteria
The teacher uses very few exemplification materials	The teacher uses clear examples so that the children understand what they are trying to achieve
Teachers give children little time to think about their learning	Teachers build in opportunities for learners to think about and discuss their learning
Children rarely review work	Children are prepared to improve work after reflection and discussion
The teacher identifies strengths and weaknesses in children's work	Learners share responsibility for evaluating learning outcomes
After the lesson	
Marking of work is superficial, gives only general praise or uses grades/marks	Marking is constructive and helps learners understand how they can improve
Children read teachers' written feedback but do not act on it	Children use written feedback to improve work
Children move quickly to the next lesson	Previous learning is recalled and links with present learning are established. Time to revisit and improve work is given
Teachers use tests to take snapshots of children's progress	On-going use of evidence to help learners decide where they are now and what they need to do next
Periodic end-of-unit tests provide main source of assessment data	Day-to-day assessment strategies are used by teachers and learners

In this section we look at how we might use assessment evidence to help children improve in reading. The flow chart below gives a general overview of children's development. We also look at each assessment focus in turn; in particular at how to assess children's development and help them move through National Curriculum Levels. Finally, we consider how to set appropriate progress targets to help children improve their skills in reading.

Using *Assessment* to help children learn

If we are to use assessment to help children make better progress in reading, we need to be aware of the necessary SKILLS and UNDERSTANDING required for each Reading Assessment Focus.

Some Assessment Focuses, e.g. AFs 2, 4 and 5, lend themselves more readily to direct teaching, whereas others depend more on the provision of appropriate opportunities for developing reading experience.

Generally, children follow the same pattern of progress when engaging with texts and becoming better readers, as shown in the flow chart below.

How children develop as readers

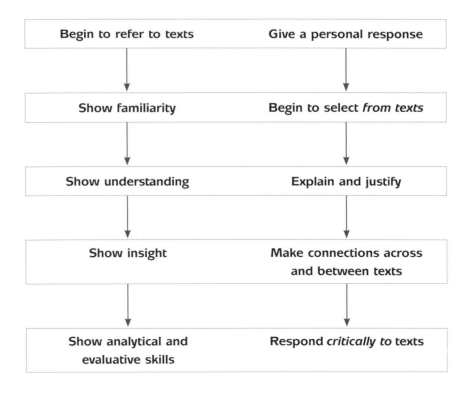

Progression in the Primary National Strategy Framework for Teaching Literacy

In the Framework, progression in reading is not shown in terms of progress through Assessment Focuses. Instead Strands 5, 7 and 8 identify 'a clear set of outcomes for learning progression' in each year in reading.

Strand 5 concentrates on the skills and understanding associated with Assessment Focus 1 – word reading skills and strategies.

Strand 7 covers Assessment Focuses 2 to 5 under the heading 'Understanding and Interpreting texts'.

Strand 8 includes Assessment Focus 6 within a set of learning objectives which emphasise independence and enjoyment of reading. Assessment Focus 7 appears in Year 6 in this Strand.

The progression identified within the Framework for Literacy is broadly in line with the Assessment Focuses which are set out in much greater detail below.

Recognising children's performance at each level and moving them on to the next

The following level-by-level guides to Assessment Focuses 2–7 give a broad outline of children's performance at each level. Note that a child may well display characteristics of more than one level in any single piece of work.

Assessment Focus 2: Understand, describe, select or retrieve information, events or ideas from texts and use quotation and reference to text

Level by level guide

LEVEL 2

At Level 2 children:
- can read and understand simple questions
- find and retrieve information from a specific point in the text
- scan a text slowly to find key words
- sequence two/three events
- identify an obvious similarity or difference between texts, e.g. opening/ending
- look back to the text when giving simple explanations
- generate their own simple questions about one specific point in texts
- give reasons for events
- summarise a text with a simple recount

Moving children on

To move from Level 2 to Level 3 teachers should ensure that children:
- read a wider range of unfamiliar texts
- underline key words in questions
- look back to, and use information in texts to answer questions
- search for information at more than one point in a text
- practise scanning a text more quickly to find key words (see 'Fastest Finger First', PCM 3, page 38)
- observe the teacher modelling reading for different purposes
- are taught how to find information quickly and accurately using organisational features of non-fiction texts, e.g. index, contents
- are shown how to use quotation marks when using quotations.

LEVEL 3

At Level 3 children:

- take note of particular instructions or key words in questions, e.g. page numbers, references to specific paragraphs
- scan a larger text more quickly to find key words or phrases
- read in different ways depending on the task, e.g. read instructions word for word, reread for accuracy or skim read a magazine looking for topics of interest
- refer to more than one specific point in the text when giving explanations
- begin to use quotations but often copy more text than needed
- make use of alphabetically ordered indexes and other features in non-fiction texts, e.g. headings, contents to find information
- make notes when collecting information but rely mainly on copying.

LEVEL 4

At Level 4 children:

- tailor answers to questions, e.g. understand that 'how' and 'why' questions need to be tackled differently
- understand some test question words, e.g. sequence, compare
- can sequence 4/5 events
- pick out similarities and differences in longer texts
- select quotations appropriately
- generate questions about whole texts independently
- find information confidently, using more than one source and a range of research strategies
- annotate texts with simple notes
- summarise texts in detail.

LEVEL 5

At Level 5 children:

- understand a range of questions and the reading requirements for all assessment focuses
- understand a wide range of question words, e.g. effective, summary
- can compare the sequence of events in more than one text
- pick out similarities/differences in more than one text and use these to support analyses of themes, characters, events etc.
- find and quote key words from several points in texts to support opinions and explanations
- generate more sophisticated questions about texts and use a wide range of source material confidently to collate information
- make succinct and pertinent notes when finding information and acknowledge sources.

To move from Level 3 to Level 4 teachers should ensure that, in addition to the statements above, children:

- read a wide range of texts
- think about the Assessment Focus when answering questions (see page 31)
- understand test question words e.g. 'feature' and 'function' (see page 46)
- sequence 4/5 events correctly
- select text appropriately to use in quotations and for note making
- have opportunities for independent research using more than one source.

To move from Level 4 to Level 5 teachers should ensure that, in addition to the statements above, children:

- have the opportunity to read a range of more challenging texts
- understand how to answer a full range of questions confidently
- find quotations quickly and use them confidently to support explanations
- practise selecting relevant information to enable them to compare texts
- have the opportunity to carry out research when answering own questions using a range of source materials and using note-taking skills appropriately.

Assessment Focus 3: Deduce, infer and interpret information, events or ideas from texts

Level by Level guide

LEVEL 2

At Level 2 children:

- give a general personal response to actions, events and characters, e.g. 'I would feel sad if that happened …'
- make predictions based on the text
- make reasonable inferences from clear statements in the text, e.g. 'I think it is winter because it says "icy pavements"' (see 'Cool and Uncool Guesses' page 41).

LEVEL 3

At Level 3 children:

- comment on actions, events and characters using simple references to text not just personal response
- begin to explain their own interpretations of character, motives, events and ideas using the text (See 'Cool and Uncool Guesses' page 41)
- recognise the differences between fact and opinion
- recognise obvious themes in a text, e.g. 'it's about people who all feel lonely'.

LEVEL 4

At Level 4 children:

- use a range of textual clues to comment on character, motives, events and ideas (See 'Cool and Uncool Guesses' page 41)
- show understanding of character, motives, events and ideas through more detailed explanations and predictions
- identify both explicit and implicit messages in texts
- speculate using the text for support.

LEVEL 5

At Level 5 children:

- use a full range of evidence across texts to comment on and show understanding of characters, motives, events and ideas
- justify own opinions, preferences and predictions using a range of contextual clues
- comment on explicit and implicit aspects of a text
- understand underlying themes and viewpoints.

Moving children on

To move children from Level to Level in AF3 teachers need to:

- encourage children to respond to, predict, comment on and justify opinions using an *increasingly wide range of texts*
- teach children to use *a greater number of textual clues* to support their opinions
- help children to *identify and understand themes*
- teach children to recognise *implied as well as explicit meaning* in texts.

Assessment Focus 4: Identify and comment on the structure and organisation of texts including grammatical and presentational features at text level

Level by Level guide

LEVEL 2

At Level 2 children:

- use alphabetically ordered texts, e.g. index
- in non-fiction books find and use named features, e.g. contents
- identify a range of punctuation in texts.

LEVEL 3

At Level 3 children:

- recognise the main organisational features of different text types
- give simple explanations of how organisational features help the reader in non-fiction texts, e.g. the arrows show you which way round the life cycle you go; the glossary tells you what words mean
- find and select information using a range of organisational features, e.g. headings, captions, sub-headings
- give simple explanations about the use of punctuation in texts.

LEVEL 4

At Level 4 children:

- name a wider range of organisational features and explain their function
- link organisational features to the purpose of the text
- identify structural similarities and differences between texts
- explain the purpose of a range of punctuation
- understand and comment on how texts are presented for effect
- recognise how paragraphs and ideas within paragraphs are linked, e.g. connectives and reference chains (different words used to refer to the same thing or idea, e.g. 'dog', 'animal', 'pet').

LEVEL 5

At Level 5 children:

- name a full range of organisational features and explain their function
- compare and evaluate different types of text organisation and structure
- explain the purpose of a full range of grammatical features and punctuation
- explain how print, images and sound are combined to create meaning
- link the ways in which writers of non-fiction use language and organisational features to writers' purpose.

Moving children on

To move children from Level to Level in AF4 teachers need to:

- ensure that children read an *increasingly wide range of texts* of different text types and *evaluate their structure and organisation*
- teach children the names and function of *an increasing range of organisational features*
- teach children how to use organisational features of non-fiction texts to *carry out research efficiently*
- teach children the purpose of an *increasingly wide range of punctuation*
- encourage children to identify ways in which writers *use grammatical features to structure texts*, e.g. connectives and paragraph links.

Assessment Focus 5: Explain and comment on writers' use of language, including grammatical and literary features at word and sentence level

Level by Level guide

LEVEL 2

At Level 2 children:
- pick out simple well-chosen words
- recognise simple patterns, e.g. repeated words, rhymes, familiar openings
- develop an understanding of simple unfamiliar words by using clues in the text, e.g. using pictures and other nearby words.

LEVEL 3

At Level 3 children:
- identify words, e.g. 'find two words which describe her fast movement'
- begin to understand why writers use particular words and explain their understanding in general terms, e.g. 'he is trying to make us laugh'
- link writers' choice of words to the purpose and type of text, e.g. 'he uses these science words because it's all about Space'
- develop an understanding of words by making links with other familiar words, word roots etc.

LEVEL 4

At Level 4 children:
- identify and explain more difficult unfamiliar words by using a range of contextual clues, e.g. the rest of the sentence or references within paragraphs
- identify writers' use of imagery or comparisons and make simple interpretations
- give more precise explanations for why writers use particular words, e.g. '"catastrophic" is a powerful word to use because it tells you just how terrible it is going to be'
- work out how the same word can have different meanings in different contexts.

LEVEL 5

At Level 5 children:
- work out the meaning of specialist words by using a full range of contextual clues across whole texts
- explain how and why writers use words in figurative language
- explain how and why writers use words to affect a reader's thoughts and feelings
- explain words and phrases with double meanings
- comment on authorial techniques and style and recognise how writers combine different techniques to create a particular mood or effect.

Moving children on

To move children from Level to Level in AF5 teachers need to:
- give children practice at *finding words* with a particular meaning
- encourage children to make collections of words with similar meanings
- during reading, allow children to 'rob' examples of well-chosen words or phrases for their 'Robbery Books'
- give children *practice in working out unknown words*
- teach children *how to interpret* comparisons, puns and other figurative language
- *discuss writers' techniques and style* using increasingly sophisticated examples.

Assessment Focus 6: Identify and comment on writers' purposes and viewpoints, and the overall effect of the text on the reader

Level by Level guide

LEVEL 2

At Level 2 children:

- give a simple personal response to a piece of writing, e.g. 'I like it because it's funny'
- make choices between texts giving simple reasons
- recognise writers' viewpoints in simple terms, e.g. 'he doesn't like ...'
- know the difference between main types of text, e.g. fiction/non-fiction, story/playscript.

LEVEL 3

At Level 3 children:

- express opinions and explain their preferences
- explain simply what a writer is trying to achieve, e.g. 'she's trying to say you should buy it'
- use the whole text to summarise a writer's viewpoint in simple terms
- compare different versions of the same text
- explore preferences by choosing texts of a certain type, or by a favourite author.

LEVEL 4

At Level 4 children:

- express opinions and justify preferences based on more experience of a wider range of reading material
- identify the writer's main purpose(s) for writing the text
- explain writers' viewpoint(s)
- use specific points in a text to explain the effect on the reader
- compare how a common theme is developed in different texts, e.g. how bullying is depicted in two poems, or how writers' views about animals are developed in a poem, leaflet and newspaper article.

LEVEL 5

At Level 5 children:

- read and engage with an extensive range of material, explaining and justifying preferences to other readers
- identify independently and comment on key aspects of a fiction text as a basis for critical analysis, e.g. character, themes, plot development
- recognise techniques used by writers, e.g. to persuade and analyse the success of a text against its purpose
- explain and comment on how a particular viewpoint is developed
- use an overview of the text supported by specific examples from several points to explain the effect on the reader.

Moving children on

To move children from Level to Level in AF6 teachers need to:

- guide children to *read a wider variety of material* and to express *preferences for authors and genres*
- encourage *discussion between readers* so that children have the opportunity to hear other readers explain views
- give children the opportunity to read material centred on *common themes*
- use *model texts* to make explicit the *links* between the *purpose and effect of writers' work* and children's own writing
- encourage children to analyse texts through the appropriate (i.e. not every time children read or every text they read) *use of reading journals/diaries*.

Assessment Focus 7: Relate texts to their social, cultural and historical traditions

Level by Level guide

LEVEL 2

At Level 2 children:
- understand that books describe people, times and settings in both familiar and unfamiliar contexts
- know the main differences between types of fiction and non-fiction texts, e.g. stories, fact books.

LEVEL 3

At Level 3 children:
- make simple observations about individual writers, e.g. 'he writes lots of football stories'
- make simple observations about the setting, characters etc., e.g. 'it starts in an old-fashioned school.'

LEVEL 4

At Level 4 children:
- focus on a particular writer identifying similarities between books, e.g. 'he often writes animal stories. The animals always get into trouble'
- make points about the parts that social, cultural or historical contexts play in a story, e.g. 'because it's in London during World War 2, this makes life dangerous for the boy in the story'.

LEVEL 5

At Level 5 children
- compare how writers from different times and places present experiences and use language
- comment critically and compare the styles of different writers
- begin to understand the importance of individual books/writers in our literary heritage and some aspects of literary traditions, e.g. the popularity and themes of Superhero comic strips.

Moving children on

To move children from Level to Level in AF7 teachers need to:
- use questions to draw out children's responses to, and understanding of, *social, cultural and historical issues in books*
- provide *information about individual writers*, e.g. biographies, film, Internet and collections of their work to enable children to form opinions about their writing.

The following simple targets concentrate on key areas of reading. They are not intended to cover each level comprehensively, but instead provide teachers and children with the practical guidance they need to make progress from level to level. They are intended to be used primarily as *lesson objectives* in other subject areas, but you could, of course, use them in Literacy lessons as well.

Using *progress targets* to move children from level to level

Depending on the context, choose an *appropriate* reading target and introduce it as an objective for your lesson, together with any other subject specific lesson objectives. You do not need to cover the objectives in any systematic way, but putting a dot or tick next to each target addressed in this way will help to show you any gaps in coverage.

As a result, over the course of a term, you will continually revisit key reading skills in a meaningful cross-curricular context. Children also begin to appreciate the value of reading as they apply their developing skills in other curriculum areas. At the end of term, you are able to see which targets you have taught and which you can plan to include next.

So they can also be used in Literacy lessons, the targets are listed under the appropriate level. However, in cross-curricular work, levels of readers and of targets can be ignored. Instead, select just one appropriate target for the lesson you are delivering, and use it as a class objective for all children.

What is important is that during the course of the lesson you explicitly teach the skills and understanding associated with your chosen target.

Example: Organisation of information texts

In science you tell the children that they will be learning all about the life cycle of the butterfly and how the butterfly changes at various stages of its life.

You explain that the other objective of the lesson is to learn how texts are organised to help readers find information easily.

During the lesson, you draw attention to the importance of the arrows in guiding readers round the diagram of the life cycle, the ways in which captions underneath photographs of each stage explain to readers how the butterfly changes and how the short glossary gives the meaning of specialist words in the text. You point out that the words in the glossary are in bold black font to make them stand out to the reader and to separate them from the definition.

Children might be given the opportunity to explain to each other, using a different text, the function of these particular organisational features.

During the plenary, knowledge and understanding of both science and reading objectives is consolidated and evaluated.

Progress Targets

Targets are given below, with ideas for implementation in cross-curricular lessons (where applicable) in brackets.

To help me to move from Level 2 to Level 3, here are my main targets:	
1 Read unseen pieces of writing accurately (All lessons)	☐
2 Pick out things that are the same and different in two story endings, two story openings or two factual pieces of writing (Geography – Comparing descriptions of life in two places, e.g. a village and a city)	☐
3 Look back to and use the text when I am explaining what it is about (All lessons)	☐
4 Explain why characters behave, think and feel as they do (Literacy)	☐
5 Work out why things happen in the story and predict what I think will happen next (Literacy)	☐
6 Recognise and use parts of fact books which help me to find information, e.g. contents, index, glossary, main headings, sub-headings, captions (History – using sources of information to find out about the lives of significant historical figures)	☐
7 Use my knowledge of the alphabet to find a word quickly in a dictionary, glossary or thesaurus (Modern Foreign Languages – finding the meanings of words) (Science – using a glossary to find the meaning of scientific terms in a study of insects)	☐
8 Begin to understand why writers use particular words (e.g. are they trying to make us laugh, describe a place, persuade us to do something, make us feel sorry for someone?) (PSHCE – reading a child's account of a bullying incident and identifying language used by the writer to develop empathy)	☐

To help me to move from Level 3 to Level 4, here are my main targets:

1 Pick out important command words in questions/instructions and make sure that my answer does as the question says
(Maths – finding consecutive numbers with a product or total of 'x')
(P.E. – reading instructions in order to play a small-sided game)
(D & T – following instructions for making a model) ☐

2 Use a writer's words to back up my answers
(History – use quotations to support opinions, e.g. that the Aztec city of Tenochtitlan impressed the Spanish/that children in Victorian factories were treated badly)
(Maths or Science – use phrases from probability questions or statements about experiments to explain reasoning, e.g. I know that the spinners cannot show 'a total of more than 8' because Spinner A 'only has numbers 3 and below' and …) ☐

3 Pick out similarities and differences in two pieces of writing
(History – compare two versions of the same event) ☐

4 Identify the main points of a piece of writing
(History – present the events which led to the start of World War 2 as a timeline; explain why the Greek trireme was so successful in battle)
(Geography – summarise the way places are linked to one another, e.g. by trade)
(Science – draw a labelled diagram of a life cycle from factual information) ☐

5 Work out the order of events/ideas in a piece of writing
(D & T– rearrange jumbled instructions into a logical, step-by-step plan of how to make a biscuit box) ☐

6 Work out hidden meanings in a text (See 'Cool and Uncool Guesses' page 41)
(History – reading an ambassador's account of a visit to the court of a Tudor monarch, what is being implied?)
(R.E. – work out the message in Jesus' parables) ☐

7 Work out what words in the writing mean by using a dictionary or glossary, or by reading the rest of the sentence or paragraph
(Any subject where specialist vocabulary is introduced) ☐

8 Know what a writer is trying to make me think
(PHSCE – that smoking is bad for our health or that keeping animals in zoos is vital for endangered species) ☐

To help me to move from Level 4 to Level 5, here are my main targets:	
1 Find key sentences and phrases at different points in a text to support my opinions (History – non-chronological report 'What the Ancient Greeks Have Done for Us' using quotations from research into the achievements and influence of Greek civilisation)	☐
2 Explain the main ideas of a piece of writing; compare the main ideas in two pieces of writing (History – two contrasting accounts of children's lives in Victorian times from a factory owner and Lord Shaftsbury)	☐
3 Work out characters' motives, feelings etc., using a range of clues from different points in the text, e.g. dialogue, actions and descriptions (Literacy)	☐
4 Understand why different texts are set out as they are and consider how successful they are in terms of layout (Geography – Environment topic: Compare the effectiveness of a table of information about endangered and vulnerable whales with two paragraphs with sub-headings about the same topic)	☐
5 Understand how writers use words to affect readers' thoughts and feelings (Geography – articles which explain how people can damage or improve the environment and how our actions can affect the future quality of people's lives)	☐
6 Work out abbreviations and specialist words using the sentence, paragraph or text where they occur (History – using archive material, e.g. newspaper reports) (Geography – water cycle)	☐
7 Understand ways in which writers present issues in fiction and non-fiction; recognise the writer's point of view (Geography – Changing Land Use topic: Considering statements of, for example, a farmer, tourist, water board official and a naturalist about proposals to flood a valley to create a new reservoir)	☐
8 Explain how different texts have different purposes (ICT – sharing and exchanging information in a variety of forms)	☐

Other uses of progress targets

In addition, you and your children can use the simplified progress targets above in the following more conventional ways:

1 After marking optional tests, teachers in Years 3, 4 and 5 identify <u>personal reading targets</u> for individuals or groups of children.

2 From Year 6 children's completed past test papers, teachers identify weaker areas by analysing mistakes and setting targets to <u>support focused revision</u>.

3 Children use these targets, which have been written in simple terms, to help them <u>evaluate their own progress</u> in AfL activities.

4 Teachers use them as <u>group objectives</u> in Guided Reading sessions.

Using PROGRESS to set individual improvement targets

You need to consider the following principles when setting individual improvement targets for children in reading.

P.   R.   O.   G.   R.   E.   S.   S.

Personal profile

Children generally work at one level in reading, but each child will have an individual profile with strengths and weaknesses in different areas. Often teachers find this uneven profile easier to identify in writing than reading simply because evidence is more readily available. If we are to set improvement targets in reading we need to make them pertinent to each child's particular needs. This means that we must have a good grasp of progression in each Assessment Focus (see pages 12–18) where detailed lists will help you to identify where the child is now and where he/she needs to be.

Relevant texts

Not all texts lend themselves to work with a particular Assessment Focus.

So that children do not become demoralised because the same individual improvement targets are dragging on for too long with little or no opportunity to make progress, make sure that they work with appropriate texts on appropriate tasks. This can be addressed in the following ways:

- Guided Reading groups can be flexible to accommodate children whose targets are similar
- reading journal tasks can be adapted to meet the needs of each improvement target
- a child might work on a particular 'Reading Solo' (see PCMS 11–13, pages 61–63)
- discussion with the child about his/her current reading book can be engineered to include relevant questions (see 'PCM 20, Fiction Brainteasers' page 70)
- Story sack work can be organised so that different tasks concentrate on different Assessment Focuses. Story sacks contain a book, together with a range of associated reading and writing activities from which children make a selection for working on at home. The story sack is then passed on to another child.

Optimum number

Clearly, the number of targets for each child can depend on such things as the child's ability, attitude and rate of progress. The nature of the targets set might also determine how many we give children at any one time. Generally speaking, children should have no more than three, but even then, children can suffer from 'target fatigue' if we are not careful, especially when we consider they may also have targets for writing and maths. Consider setting only one individual improvement target in reading. This makes the process more manageable and progress more likely.

 Giving a guarantee

When setting a target make it explicit to children what they have to do and how/when they need to do it so that progress will be made. The more you believe that success is guaranteed, the more confidence you will inspire and the more easily the target will be met.

 Review

Finding time to review individual improvement targets is difficult, to say the least. Make use of post-it notes or annotations on work to jot down evidence as and when you discuss reading with children, or when marking written evidence in all areas of the curriculum. The more children are involved in their own target setting and the more they understand their particular target, the easier it becomes to review progress. Discussion with reading partners enables them to reflect on their own progress. Also encourage them to carry out neat highlighting in margins to show where evidence can be found.

 Evidence

Evidence in reading can be found in many different places and can be presented in many different forms. Although comprehension-type exercises can provide a snapshot of a child's progress they also limit the child's opportunity to show the full extent of their understanding because of the closed nature of the task. (See 'Leave no stone unturned', pages 25–27.)

 Small steps

Break down each target into manageable chunks to show children exactly how and what they are going to need to do. (See pages 20–22.) Group children whenever possible so that they can help each other assess progress.

 Simple

Keep individual improvement targets as simple and practical as possible.
Choose KEY targets for each level and stick to these to make the process manageable. (See pages 20–22 for 'small-steps' pro-formas.)

> *Example:*
>
> *My target is – to identify the main points in a piece of writing.*
>
> *Over the next four weeks read one (or two, or three) different types of text:*
>
> **1** *An account of how Jenner developed vaccine*
> **2** *A newspaper report about a motorway accident*
> **3** *A balanced argument about whether school uniform should be banned*
>
> ▶ *Highlight events – what happened at each stage?*
> ▶ *Answer the Who? What? Where? When? and Why? questions*
> ▶ *Look at the first and last sentences in each paragraph. Pick out key phrases.*
>
> *For each piece of writing, show and tell a Reading Buddy the main points. Record or stick highlighted evidence in your books. Tick and date target sheet.*

This section includes lots of practical ideas for ongoing assessment of children's reading, including suggestions for ways to prepare children for SATs-type questions. We also look at ways to help children with specific problems and issues through a series of 'Reading Clinics', as well as how to support children of different abilities through differentiated tasks.

Assessment of *reading* in practice

Many teachers find it difficult to collect evidence to support assessments in reading. There are, in fact, many ways to do this in the Key Stage 2 classroom, each with its own benefits and limitations. Below are examples of the many classroom activities we can use to find evidence of attainment and progress in reading.

Leave no stone unturned

1 **Comprehension** exercises are useful because children are usually able to work independently, especially if questions are differentiated. They provide a written form of evidence that can be marked and assessed later, as well as a record of particular difficulties. Comprehension books also include questions on all Assessment Focuses and a range of different text types. They are of limited value because it is sometimes difficult to establish the extent of children's understanding from their written responses (which are often as short as possible!). Some children are discouraged by the amount of writing entailed and others find the work repetitive and tedious after a while.

2 **Guided reading** sessions provide a valuable opportunity to focus on particular aspects of reading with groups, or individual children within a group. When children read and discuss texts, our understanding of their strengths and weaknesses is more comprehensive. Oral, as opposed to written questions, are more flexible and enable us to assess the extent of children's understanding, adapting our teaching and questioning accordingly. Once the teacher has modelled the process, children can also be given the responsibility of leading the group as it predicts, reads, questions and summarises a text, section by section. Some teachers find practical problems interfere with the smooth running of guided reading. To help with this:

- give each child an organisational role and train them to collect and distribute resources efficiently so that time is not wasted

- complete a simple record of where each group is and what they will do next at the end of each session

- make use of extra adults, ICT facilities and relevant research tasks to give every group appropriate challenges

- use teacher-friendly ways of recording the contributions of individual children, e.g. Talkpods, sticky notes, group records (see PCM 21, page 71)

3 Children's on-going **record of books read** or library borrowing habits enable us to judge the breadth and depth of their reading. To be able to discuss AF7 issues and make judgements, teachers might encourage children to read more of the same author, or make suggestions of alternatives to help them develop wider reading tastes.

4. **Hearing children read** helps us to assess their fluency, expression, phonic knowledge, understanding of the role of punctuation and their use of syntax, context, word origins and structures to make sense of the text. It is also a shared experience and facilitates questioning (PCM 20, page 70 for 'Fiction Brainteasers' and page 31 for questions related to particular Assessment Focuses.)

5. **Reading journals** tell us a great deal about children as independent readers, their understanding of texts and their preferences. They provide evidence for judgements in all Assessment Focuses and enable more able children especially to respond personally to texts.

6. **Story sacks** allow children to work independently and exercise some choice in the way they respond to books. Teachers can adapt activities to suit different Assessment Focuses.

7. Teachers can set up **'Big Buddy'** reading (an older reader paired up with a younger 'buddy'). The experienced reader listens to the 'Buddy' reading, and discusses issues relating to the text.

8. The use of appropriate **artefacts, costumes or 'props'** often draws out original responses to texts. Children might talk about their significance in the book, imagine that they are talking from the object's point of view, summarise the story or make predictions.

9. Teachers can use children's **independent research** to make judgements on their use of source material, knowledge of organisational features and ability to summarise and interpret information.

10. Readers need to create mental pictures while they are reading. Visual **representations** of text support understanding and can be as varied as the texts themselves. These visual interpretations are valuable evidence for assessment purposes, e.g. a child can produce a flow chart summary of a writer's argument. Story boards with captions, mind maps, labelled photofit pictures of characters, diagrams, timelines, models, book jackets, photographs and filmed drama sequences are some of the many visual ways to explore understanding in reading.

11. **Reading transformations** (where the original content is turned into another form, e.g. a holiday advert into a postcard home or a narrative poem into a diary) encourage children to interpret texts in interesting and creative ways.

12. **Drama** (including such activities as role playing scenes/characters, hot-seating of characters or the author, giving advice in Conscience Alley) can provide evidence of children's ability to analyse characters' feelings and motives.

13. **Writing a letter** to the author, or writing as the author can help teachers to assess children's understanding of viewpoint and purpose.

14 Teaching children that in reading, good questions can be as valuable as good answers, encourages them to actively engage with texts and become more independent readers. When they devise **their own questions** (PCM 11, page 61) we can assess their ability to select, explore and prioritise issues in texts.

15 **Reading 'Solos'** (PCMs 11–13, pages 61–63) encourage children to work more independently as readers and, more importantly, to think about texts in a structured way without being provided with too much support. Because 'Solos' sheets are generic and involve more than just comprehension-type activities, teachers should model them with the whole class using a class reader. 'Solos' can be used flexibly either as one-off activities or put together in a booklet providing either a predetermined weekly programme of work for guided reading groups or a carousel of activities from which children/teachers can choose.

It can take up to half a term of modelling for children to become confident, but, once embedded, 'Solos' can be used with any book. They improve children's ability to organise their work in guided reading, so that they can respond as readers with increasing confidence. They are also useful in assessment terms because they show evidence of independent rather than supported reading.

16 From **classroom observations** we can note how children select material, discuss material and read alone in sustained reading sessions.

17 Teachers might annotate children's **book reviews**. They might also record or make notes on children's presentations of 'A Brilliant Book' to assess how well they select points, summarise and engage with books.

18 Observations of children **reading in other curriculum areas** will show whether children read for different purposes, e.g. close step-by-step reading of an instruction text or scanning and selective reading of a newspaper.

19 **D.A.R.T.S.** (Directed activities related to texts), e.g. text analysis, highlighting and sequencing can provide plenty of evidence of readers' ability to interrogate a text.

20 **Tests** give us a standardised level for each reader but an analysis of responses to individual questions can also highlight strengths and weaknesses in particular Assessment Focuses.

Giving children the tools for the job

It helps if children have a basic understanding of all seven Assessment Focuses in reading. Explain that to be a good reader children need to read in lots of different ways. At different times using different texts, give children examples of questions from particular assessment focuses as part of your day-to-day shared reading. Explain in simple terms what each AF requires. Devise a phrase and action for each one to help children remember the differences. Use these in shared and guided reading to remind children what they need to do.

AF2: I can find answers in the text.

Sound: WOOF! WOOF!

Action: Both hands retrieving an imaginary 'answer bone'.

AF3: I can infer and deduce things from clues in the text.

Sound: HMMMMM.......

Action: Holding the magnifier and moving it back and forth.

AF4: I can talk about how texts are set out and organised.

Sound: SORT IT! SORT IT!

Action: Using index fingers children draw a rectangle and point to imaginary features.

AF5: I can think and explain how the writer has used words to make the text more powerful.

Sound: GABBLE! GABBLE!

Action: Point to head, then mouth with action to show words rolling out.

AF6: I can comment on a writer's viewpoint and how a text makes a reader feel.

Sound: WRITE! WRITE! YIPPEE! BOO HOO!

Action: Children use thumbs and fingers to make spectacles around the eyes, pretend to write, then make a smiley face and sad face.

AF7: I can link books to their time and place and compare books by the same writer and different writers.

Sound: First bar of 'Dr. Who' time travel tune.

Action: Press buttons and pull levers to move to a different time and place.

To engage with a text, readers need to be able to speculate about events, ideas, characters' feelings, motives and actions, and to ask themselves questions while reading. The simple suggestions below help children to do this.

Helping children to formulate their own questions

1 *True or false?*

Using a familiar text and different assessment focuses put three or four questions on the board. At the start of the lesson, pairs of children, one with FALSE and the other with TRUE written on whiteboards, spend five minutes discussing the questions, ready to hold up the appropriate answer when the time is up and the teacher asks the whole class for opinions.

2 *Teach children sounds and actions for each Assessment Focus.* (pages 28–29)

Using questions (page 31) ask children to identify the Assessment Focus, carry out the action and make the sound. (More able children might think correctly that some questions are drawn from more than one assessment focus, and this is a useful discussion point.)

3 *Think of a question*

Using a factual text, children think of questions that arise from it and then carry out further research to find answers.

4 *If this is the answer… what would the question be?*

With a familiar text, put answers on the board. In pairs, children write down possible questions for each one on whiteboards.

5 *Birthday 'brainies' and 'bloomers'*

Tell children that good questions are as important as good answers. Help them to differentiate between open and closed questions, good questions (brainies) and not so good questions (bloomers) which require only very simple answers. Use good 'Question Solos' (see PCM 11, page 61) or research questions and display brilliant examples around a Cup Winner's medal or birthday cake.

'Congratulations! You have thought of some GREAT questions!'

Examples of questions for each Assessment Focus

AF2	AF3
What happened before/after/when …? Which word/phrase/paragraph tells us …? Draw a timeline of what happened … Describe … Write down one reason why … Find and copy … How are … same/different? Who/where/when/why/what/how did …? Which event …? Give two ways … Draw lines to link … Who/where/when/why/what/how are …? Name two important things about … Decide which statements are true/false.	Give one reason why … What does this tell you about …? Why did/does …? What is important about …? What will happen …? What do the words … tell us about … feelings? How does … feel about …? How do you know that …? What was different after …? What were … thoughts when …? How do you know? What is the writer describing? Use the information to think of a title/headings. What did … mean by saying …? What clues are there that …?
AF4	**AF5**
What do the arrows/lines/labels show? Why is the text presented like this? What is the function (job) of the …? Which feature (part) does …? Why are the captions/diagrams important? How do the … help the reader? What is the purpose of the question mark/exclamation marks/ellipsis? How does the layout help the reader? How does the writer use … connectives? Why is a different font used for the …?	Why are the words … used? Why does the writer compare … to …? What do the words … make you think? What is their effect? What is the effect of putting words in this order? How do the words used make us feel …?
AF6	**AF7**
Which poem/fact box/article do you prefer and why? Which style of writing do you prefer and why? The story/poem/paragraph is about … Do you agree? Explain your reasons. Do you agree with the writer that …? How does the writer tell us that … and … are similar/different? Why does the writer include …? What message is the writer giving? Does the writer like …? How do you know?	Which title/type of writing best describes the story? Which other stories/poems by this writer have you read? Are there similarities/differences? Which do you prefer and why? Is the writing 'true to life'? Explain your reasons.

The poem 'Girl Power' by Les Baynton describes a scene familiar to most children. The poem provides scope for stimulating discussion, role play and interesting interpretations. You can use selected activities from the ideas below to address particular Assessment Focuses. Suggestions are also suitable for use with other poems. *See PCM 23, page 73 for a peer/self-assessment sheet 'Responding to Poetry'.*

Helping children read & respond to poetry

Planning overview

You may find the following suggestions useful to develop children's understanding of themes, structure and use of language in poetry. The poem also provides an excellent stimulus for speaking and listening activities and for helping children to produce quality written work. If you decide to video children working, it is useful to set this up early in the process so that children are used to being filmed.

- Introduce the poem with the title and last line removed (see PCM 1, page 33).
  Title: Girl Power
  Last line: 'And the King seems a little smaller'

- Read the poem to the children (a confident girl might be asked to read the parts in capitals).

- Children read the poem to themselves and, at the end, highlight something in the poem that they had not noticed the first time. They share these with a POETRY PARTNER. Although not essential, it is helpful to have boy/girl poetry partners for this particular poem. (**AF2**)

- Children write down a suitable title and last line for the poem and then explain their choices to their poetry partner. A class discussion of choices might follow. At this point the teacher groups suggested titles under main headings to develop children's understanding of the poem's themes. (**AF6**)

- Children work on VIEWPOINT. One child picks out an event in the poem and exaggerates to make it seem as heroic as possible, i.e. from the character's point of view. The other makes a statement about the event from a teacher's point of view making it seem as ordinary as possible (**AF3**)
  e.g. HEROIC: The King was playing for England and scored the winning, unstoppable goal against crack opposition.
  ORDINARY: Some lads were messing around with a ball in the playground.

Name _____ Class _____

Title: _____

PCM 1 Understanding a poem

Read the poem, then see if you can think of a good title and last line for it. Write your new title and last line below.

He was King of the Playground
Lord of the Lunchbreak …
Always in the winning team,
Always first out, last back in
His voice was teacher-loud

His shouts bounced and echoed
Off the playground walls
His kicks fired the ball like a missile
Across the seething playground
And his tackles turned you over
With the force of a giant wave
All the small fry, the little fish,
Looked up at him with admiration
And a little fear

Then something happened,
One scorching summer lunchtime
With footballers all bare-chested
Like Brazilians on the beach
And girls flitting and floating
In butterfly-bright summer dresses
The King had hammered in a super goal
Hard, unstoppable … a winner all the way,
His small fans laughed and cheered
Ran to pat the wonderful back,
But one girl didn't, just his age
And just as tall, she tossed her ginger hair
Walked across the yard
And stood scowling right in front of him

YOU'VE HAD YOUR TIME …
YOUR FOOTBALL MATCH
ME AND THE GIRLS WANT TO DANCE
SO SHIFT OK

He breathed in hard, muttered something bad
And moved closer to the upstart girl
Then unflinching, she spoke in a voice just as loud as his.
I'VE TOLD YOU ONCE NOW SHIFT
ANY CLOSER AND YOU'LL GET A GREAT BIG JUICY KISS
He turned away with angry eyes
And glowing cheeks, a group of girls
Exploded the quietness into cheers and jeers

On other lunchtimes
He still struts arrogantly around,
But we all know
That something has changed.

_____

Les Baynton

- Children in pairs STORYBOARD events in the poem. Use a circular rather than a linear format. Alternatively a THOUGHT CIRCLE using thinking bubbles to record characters' thoughts and feelings during the course of the poem can be used. **(AF2, AF3)**

- A 'hot-seating' activity, with either the teacher or selected children being the King/girl, can explore characters' motives, thoughts and feelings. **(AF3)**

- With POETRY PARTNERS children 'tell the story through a sequence of mimes or freeze frames. Individual pairs may be given just one section of the poem to depict. **(AF2, AF3)**

- Children select, or are given, an appropriate section of poem to illustrate,
  e.g. 'He turned away with angry eyes and glowing cheeks'
  or, 'His voice was teacher-loud'
  or, 'All the small fry, the little fish, looked up at him with admiration.'

  Drawings, including quotations from the poem, can be arranged in order as part of a class frieze. **(AF2, AF5)**

- Children are given one section of the poem and, using a Thesaurus, find as many appropriate 'SAID' words as they can to describe how the characters might be speaking. The same activity can be done for ADVERBS. Children write out their short extract and arrange words around it, e.g:

- Children consider incidents which either happened in the poem or which are not part of the poem but MIGHT have happened, e.g.
  - the Lord of the Lunchbreak choosing sides
  - the conversation between the girls BEFORE or AFTER the incident with the boy **(AF3)**

- These incidents form the starting point for drama improvisations where children again work with poetry partners. These improvisations can either be turned into play scripts of no more than 6 lines, or into quality dialogue of no more than three lines (to include powerful 'SAID' word, adverb and action)

  e.g. *"You're dead meat," muttered the King sulkily, curling his lip.*

  "I've told you once. Now shift!" snarled the girl aggressively, putting her scowling face close to his.

- Children now work with a different poetry partner, taking it in turns to be 'director' and 'actor'. Scripts are exchanged and the 'director' has to explain how the script should be enacted. At this point, children really begin to understand why a script is laid out in a certain way. Better quality stage directions are inserted and the script can be redrafted.

- Scripts can be acted out with locations and props chosen. Scripts can then be filmed if you wish.

- This drama work can be used to assess:
  - selection and interpretation of events **(AF2)**
  - empathy with characters' feelings, motives and actions **(AF3)**
  - interpretation of writer's use of language **(AF5)**
  - understanding of writer's viewpoint and purpose **(AF6)**

- Children can draw a plot 'map' to sequence events **(AF2, AF6)**

- Children might use the 'Sense Chart' (PCM 2, page 36) to identify interesting aspects of writer's use of language – see sample below **(AF5)**

Name: Julie Smith   Class: 4B

PCM 2

Reading poetry – senses chart

You can use this chart with any poem you are reading.

From the poem find as many examples as you can for each of the headings below and complete the chart. (You may not find evidence for every heading.)

Tastes	Noises heard	Smells
juicy	shots bounced and echoed	none

Textures	Sights	Alliteration
big juicy kiss	glowing cheeks	Lord of the Lunchbreak

Simile	Metaphor	Emotions (What people think)
fired the ball like a missile	force of a giant wave	angry cheers and jeers

Name _____ Class _____

PCM 2

Reading poetry – senses chart

You can use this chart with any poem you are reading.

From the poem find as many examples as you can for each of the headings below and complete the chart. (You may not find evidence for every heading.)

Tastes	**Noises heard**	**Smells**
Textures	**Sights**	**Alliteration**
Simile	**Metaphor**	**Emotions (What people think)**

Dealing with *common problems* in children's reading

READING CLINIC 1 – Finding key words and phrases

Children need to practise horizontal and vertical scanning of texts, so play FASTEST FINGER FIRST! This is a fun but simple reading game which children never tire of and which requires no preparation.

Benefits

- Improves ability to scan texts
- Increases the speed at which children can find key words in a text

Depending on the words you choose it can also:

- introduce specialist vocabulary
- reinforce their recognition of connectives, adjectives, verbs and adverbs
- focus on particular letter strings

Organisation

- Whole class or guided reading group
- Children playing against each other in pairs (of similar reading ability)

For children who have difficulty reading, the chosen words may be pre-prepared and written on card to be uncovered one by one so that they can practise scanning without having to know how to spell the word.

Resources

Any text in any subject.

For the children's version of the game, see PCM 3, page 38.

How to play

1. The teacher identifies one paragraph of text and asks the children to read it silently.
2. Children put both hands below the desk.
3. The teacher shouts out one word (or phrase, letter string or word within a word).
4. As soon as they spot the word, children put a finger on it.
5. The teacher repeats this several times with different words.
6. The winning child is the one who scores the most 'Fastest Fingers'.

(N.B. In this game, eyes have to do the work of scanning the text. Do not allow fingers to be used early to 'circle' the text.)

Suggestions

- In Science play 'Fastest Finger' with specialist words.
- Use 'Fastest Finger' with connectives, adverbs, adjectives and other types of words.
- Play 'Fastest Finger' with a dictionary double page.
- In History use 'Fastest Finger' with key events.
- Use the index of an atlas or non-fiction book for 'Fastest Finger'.

Name _____   Class _____

PCM 3

Fastest finger first
(A game for 3 players)

1 Take a small section of text.
Two players play against each other.
The third player is the word 'setter'.

2 Both players put their hands beneath the desk or on their laps.

3 The word 'setter' chooses a word from the text and calls it out.

4 The first player to put their finger on the word wins a point.

5 This is repeated as many times as you like.
The word 'setter' keeps the score.
The winner is the player with the most points.
The winning player then becomes the word 'setter'.

6 With each new game, use a slightly larger piece of text until you can scan a whole page.

7 Do not pull your finger out until you are sure you have found the word!

For practice, read the paragraph below and then try 'Fastest Finger'.

The cat appeared from nowhere, its great golden eyes glinting as it caught sight of the foraging mouse. Meanwhile, the object of its fascination continued to nibble at the cheese, oblivious of the danger. Slowly, almost imperceptibly at first, it stiffened and then lowered its hindquarters towards the ground … crouching … waiting … ready to pounce. At first it simply wiggled its back and tail, shifting from side to side. Without taking its eyes from its prey for one second, it calculated its leap. With mounting impatience it steadied itself and … quick as a flash the small rodent caught sight of the hungry predator and dashed to safety in a small crack in the wall.

READING CLINIC 2 – Understanding key words in test questions

Suggestion 1

Throughout the school all teachers need to identify the cross-curricular lessons where the meanings of these words will be explicitly taught. This will teach children the definition but also help them to understand the word in a practical context.

All teachers should explain the meaning of the word in the same way.

Example: Teaching the word 'technique'

Curriculum area: Art
Unit: L.S. Lowry

Children watch a video about L.S. Lowry's life and work in which Lowry's technique for painting matchstick people is demonstrated.

The teacher reminds children of the key word and asks if they know the meaning. She then tells them her definition and asks them to explain the technique Lowry used.

Looking at two quite different Lowry pictures, one of boats and one of a traditional street scene, the teacher asks the children to find examples of the technique Lowry used.

In subsequent lessons, children paint a section of a Lowry scene using and adapting his technique for different figures or animals. In pairs, they explain to each other the technique they have used.

Other activities to familiarise children with the word include:

- Asking children to click fingers every time they hear the word.
- Writing the word on the board for children to look at then, covering it over, ask the children to spell it.
- How many letter 'e's does it have?
- Who can spell it backwards?
- What is the fourth letter? etc.

On each occasion, repeat the definition.

Simple definitions for the most common key words used in test questions are given below, together with suggested cross-curricular contexts for teaching them.

Word	Meaning	Curriculum area
Atmosphere	What mood does it create, e.g. peaceful, mysterious	Music – listening and responding to
Compare	Way things are different or the same	Art – comparing two paintings
Effect	Result or outcome	Science – investigating the swing of a pendulum
Feature	Part	D&T – designing a biscuit box
Function	Job	D&T – flaps on a model
Impression	Thoughts	History – what impression do you have of Henry VIII?
Purpose	Reason	D&T – cams
Sequence	Following on one from another	Maths – number sequences

Suggestion 2

Use familiar literary and media contexts to explore the meanings of these key words in quick-fire 'brain break' activities, for example:

- What is the purpose of the mirror in 'Snow White'?
- In Coronation Street, what effect did ... actions have on ...?
- What was the atmosphere in the cottage of the three bears like before and after the bears came home?

Dealing with common problems in children's reading

READING CLINIC 3 – Inference and deduction

Inference can be difficult to teach. It can be very helpful to show children a picture of an iceberg. Explain that the tip of the iceberg, the part above the water, is like the text we can see when we are reading. The part below the water line, the larger part, represents everything we can work out from studying clues in the text.

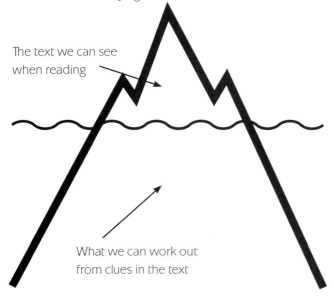

The text we can see when reading

What we can work out from clues in the text

Suggestion 1
Using cool and uncool guesses to teach inference

The following oral activity also develops children's understanding of inferential skills. Give children a short passage with your own 'guesses' attached. Children have to decide whether, given the evidence in the text, each guess is reasonable (COOL GUESS) or unreasonable because there is insufficient or contradictory evidence (UNCOOL GUESS).

These teaching principles underpin COOL and UNCOOL guesses:

1 Give the children a <u>short text</u> – no more than 4 or 5 lines. If you find these passages difficult to write, use an existing text, simplify it and attach some appropriate 'guesses'.

2 Keep the text <u>simple</u>. We are giving children practice in the <u>skills of making deductions and drawing inferences.</u>

3 <u>Give both correct and incorrect inferences.</u>

4 Ask the children to discuss the clues in pairs, but insist on a <u>text- based justification</u> not just agreement that the guesses are COOL or UNCOOL.

5 When the children are familiar with the activity, challenge them to turn an UNCOOL GUESS into a COOL GUESS by inserting a limited number of words into the simple text (e.g. make this guess a COOL GUESS using four words only. Which four words would you put into the text and where?)

6 Use flexibly, for example with a whole class in shared reading sessions, with groups in guided reading, for pair discussion (reading buddies), in other curriculum areas to support learning, or as a 'brain break'. (See page 39, Suggestion 2.)

Over the page is a teaching sequence which introduces the idea of COOL and UNCOOL guesses. It is followed by two PCMs, the first of which is for younger pupils (lower KS2), the second for older pupils (upper KS2).

Cool and uncool guesses!

Explain to children that when we read a text, some answers are easy to find because they are there on the page for us to read. Others are not so easy. We have to WORK THEM OUT by reading the words and making a good guess.

> **TOP TIPS FOR CHILDREN**
>
> 1 Always go back to the text. Do not try to answer using your general knowledge.
>
> 2 Find the key point in the text.
>
> 3 Work out an answer and then ask yourself if what you have worked out would be a reasonable guess.

The little boy was taken to hospital in an ambulance. Meanwhile the police interviewed the shocked car driver, who continually broke down in tears and pointed to the icy patch in the centre of the road. Later that day, the boy was taken home again by his parents.

Although the writing does not say so, we can work out the following from these few sentences. The words in *italics* give the clues that support the guesses.

Cool (reasonable) guesses

1 The boy was hit by a car (*little boy – ambulance – car driver*).

2 The driver was very upset about the accident (*broke down in tears*).

3 The boy was not badly hurt (*he was sent home from hospital on the same day*).

4 It was winter (*icy patch*).

Uncool (unreasonable) guesses

1 His mother was upset (*most mothers would be upset but the writing does not make this clear*).

2 It was raining (*although it may have rained to cause the ice, the writing does not make this clear*).

3 The car driver was a man (*because 'he' or 'she' is not used, we have no way of knowing if the driver was a man or not*).

PCM 4 (Lower KS2)

Cool and uncool guesses

Practise by looking at the examples below. The paragraph is followed by a number of guesses. Some are COOL guesses, i.e. reasonable ones, others are UNCOOL (unreasonable) guesses where we do not have enough information to say that the guesses are correct. If you think the guesses are reasonable, always find the part in the writing that supports your guess.

TOP TIPS

1 Always go back to the text. Do not try to answer using your general knowledge.

2 Find the key point in the text.

3 Work out an answer and then ask yourself if what you have worked out would be a reasonable guess.

The 25-year-old man hurried down the street in the rain with his hands in his pockets. His feet slipped on the icy pavement. One of his pockets bulged more than the other. He was going home for his daughter's birthday party.

Question	Cool/Uncool	Why?
1 It is winter.	Cool/Uncool	
2 He has a present for his daughter in his pocket.	Cool/Uncool	
3 He is hurrying because he has missed his bus.	Cool/Uncool	
4 He does not want to get the present wet.	Cool/Uncool	
5 He slipped because he is rushing.	Cool/Uncool	

Name _____ Class _____

PCM 5 (Upper KS2)

Cool and uncool guesses

Practise by looking at the examples below. The paragraph is followed by a number of guesses. Some are COOL guesses, i.e. reasonable ones, others are UNCOOL (unreasonable) guesses where we do not have enough information to say that the guesses are correct. If you think the guesses are reasonable, always find the part in the writing that supports your guess.

TOP TIPS

1 Always go back to the text. Do not try to answer using your general knowledge.

2 Find the key point in the text.

3 Work out an answer and then ask yourself if what you have worked out would be a reasonable guess.

After putting the correct money in the machine, they consulted the Walkers' Guide. Shortly after, they left the car park and headed up the steep track following the route carefully. Brown leaves lay in their path and far below them they could see golden trees. Puffing and panting they reached the summit from which they could see spectacular views in all directions.

Which of these guesses are COOL (reasonable) or UNCOOL (not enough evidence or evidence against)?

Question	Cool/Uncool	Why?
1 It was autumn.	Cool/Uncool	_____
2 It was an easy climb.	Cool/Uncool	_____
3 The walkers have not done this walk before.	Cool/Uncool	_____
4 It was a clear day.	Cool/Uncool	_____
5 They have arrived by train.	Cool/Uncool	_____
6 They had a good view of the lake.	Cool/Uncool	_____

Suggestion 2
Using mind mapping to teach inferential skills

Children find AF3 questions difficult. Mind maps can be used to help them retrieve, sort and use information when deducing and inferring from texts. The following model lesson also explains how to use layout to support children's learning. It is an imaginary 20-minute classroom sequence based on Question 22 – Reading Test Paper 2004.

> "…There was someone who usually noticed immediately that she wasn't around. Grandpa. Well, he used to, anyway. Things were different now…
>
> The first day he had come home from hospital she hadn't recognised the sick old man whose clothes seemed too big for him. She had pictured herself helping him get better, sorting his cushions, picking flowers for his room. She imagined him smiling and saying, 'Thank you, Fiona'. Then they would play cards and she would win most of the games. <u>But it hadn't been like that at all.</u> He sat slumped in his chair by the fire most of the day, his eyes were vague and sometimes he dribbled his food. Just like a baby!.."
>
> *What does the underlined sentence tell you about Fiona's feelings after Grandpa came out of hospital? Explain your answer fully.* <u>UP TO 3 MARKS</u>

AF3 – deduce, infer or interpret information, events or ideas from texts (complex inference).

Teacher: 'What does the question ask us to do?'
Child 1: 'Write about how Fiona feels.'
Teacher: 'Excellent. Now who will start us off by reading the underlined sentence?'
Child 2: 'But it hadn't been like that at all.'
Teacher: 'Does this tell us about how Fiona feels?'
Child 3: 'Not really.'
Teacher: 'What does it tell us?'
Child 4: 'That things have changed. They're not the same.'
Teacher: 'Can we find a phrase in the text that backs up that idea?'
Child 5: 'Things were different now.'

Children are now asked to work in pairs to find phrases which tell us what Grandpa is like now and what <u>Fiona thought</u> he would be like before he came out of hospital. The teacher guides less able readers to text <u>after</u> the underlined sentence. Strict time control is needed, e.g. 1 minute with one time check at 30 seconds to keep children on task and maintain the pace of the sequence.

Teacher: 'Time's up! Now who managed to read round the sentence to find out what Grandpa is like now and what Fiona **thought** he would be like?'

The teacher encourages contributions from three to four children, selected in order to secure inclusion of reluctant speakers, cover evidence from the whole paragraph (reinforcing the <u>before</u> and <u>after</u> position in relation to the underlined sentence), involve the hyperactive, etc.

Teacher: 'Now, is this what we were trying to explain? Look at the question again.'

Child 2: 'We were trying to explain Fiona's feelings.'

Using colour, teacher writes FIONA'S FEELINGS at the centre of a mind map on the whiteboard. In response to the question: 'How do you think she might feel because of how Grandpa has changed?', teacher writes a summary of children's responses.

It is important that <u>phrases</u> from the text are added to the mind map to reinforce skills of text reference. Quotation marks should be used to reinforce/distinguish quotes from the text.

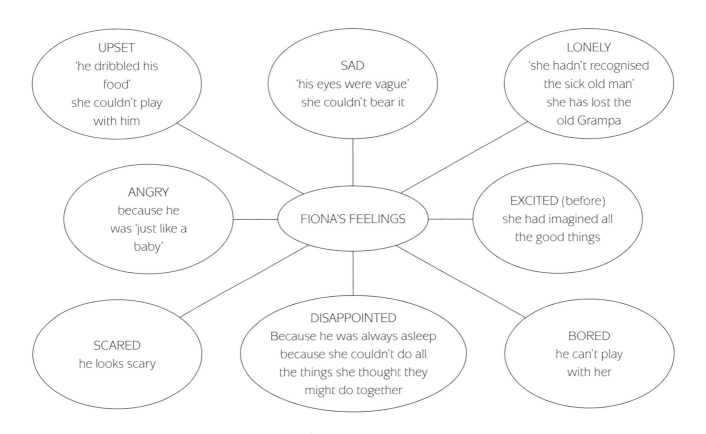

Teacher: 'That's wonderful! Now who would like to use this mind map to give us a really detailed answer to the question?'

Children: *Various responses, including extensions to peer answers.*

Teacher: 'Great! Now tell me how our answers have become better and better.'

It would now be time for the class to move on to a quite different task – but practising this sort of 'little and often' comprehension activity really underpins improved classroom performance.

Throughout this sequence, we have maintained pace and clearly focused on 'Fiona's feelings', using open-ended questions to guide children through the task. All children are involved in interrogating the text and finding and using evidence. The mind map provides visual support for children's answers while the mini-plenary gives children the opportunity to reflect on the process.

Dealing with common problems in children's reading

READING CLINIC 4 – Identifying organisational features of text and explaining their purpose

Children know through practice and experience how to use organisational features of books, e.g. contents, index and glossary. They make use of headings, sub-headings, labels and captions to find specific information. However, they find it difficult to explain the purpose, or job of each.

Until children can explain why texts are organised as they are, they find it difficult to find information quickly and also to understand fully how each feature helps the reader and why they should use similar features in their own written work.

Fun classroom activities to teach individual text features

The activities below are popular with children in KS2 and develop their knowledge and understanding of the structure and organisation of texts **(AF4)**.

1 The most useful activity of all is a very simple 5-minute '*I Spy*' game. It can be used in any lesson and is particularly good for use with cross-curricular materials, e.g. an atlas, or history, science or geography texts. The greater the variety of texts, the better – e.g. a promotional leaflet, letter, web page, table, flow chart, diagram, graph as well as written prose etc. Using the words 'feature' and 'function', set children an 'I Spy' challenge.

'I Spy, with my beautiful little eye, a feature (bit) of this text whose function (job) is to tell us what specialist words mean.'
Answer: the glossary

Teach the meaning of the words 'feature' and 'function' by asking the children to shout back 'bit' and 'job' every time they hear the words.

This activity can be used to introduce texts or provide a quick-fire 'brain break'.

Examples:

I spy with my beautiful little eye a feature (bit) of this atlas whose function (job) is to explain what the symbols on the map are.
Answer: the key

I Spy with my beautiful little eye a feature in this history book whose function is to explain what is happening in the photographs.
Answer: captions

2 Give children a list of organisational features appropriate to their reading ability, together with, if necessary, page numbers where features can be found. Children, working in pairs, imagine that their partner is an alien from Planet Zog. They must tell the alien the name of the feature, explain how to recognise it and what it does to help a reader.

3 To help children identify a range of features, give them a factual book survey (PCM 13, page 63).

4 Let pairs of children discuss 'Text features: What job does it do?' (PCM 16, page 66) or turn it into a 'Who Wants to Be a Millionaire' Game Show.

5 Design a 'job advert' for an organisational feature (PCM 19, page 69)

Give the 'job' and specific requirements (more able children can list these requirements for themselves). Children then find examples from texts or cut out examples from magazines, newspapers etc.

6 Use past test paper questions, e.g. Year 6 Reading Test 2007, Question 29.

7 'What would happen if … ?' Using a fact book children consider what would happen if a particular organisational feature was missing. Answers must refer to a specific part of the text.

Examples:
Question: *What would happen if … there wasn't an index?*
Answer: I would not be able to find out anything about the ladybird without looking at every page.

Question: *What would happen if there were no captions?*
Answer: I would not understand what Winston Churchill is doing in the photograph on page …

Question: *What would happen if there were no labels on this graph?*
Answer: I would not be able to tell how many children own cats.

Question: *What would happen if there were no arrows on the diagram?*
Answer: I would not know what happens next in the life cycle.

Dealing with common problems in children's reading

Catering for children of different abilities

We can use the same text but cater for different abilities by providing children with different levels of support. The example below, using the Year 6 2007 Reading Test Paper, shows how the same question, 'How are Volcanoes dangerous?' can be adapted. All three are based on the following extract from page 5 of the paper. Children doing levels 4–5 should also read page 7 'Disaster Strikes'.

VOLCANOES

When we hear of a volcano erupting, we think of a tall cone-shaped mountain sending out clouds of ash and liquid rock called **lava**. *In fact, volcanoes can be of different types: some are broad and flat, many are under the sea, some pour out streams of red-hot lava, some create an explosion that can be heard thousands of miles away, while others are quieter and 'gentler'.*

There are some volcanoes that can cause massive destruction although they produce little or no lava at all. The most well-known of this type is Mount Vesuvius in Italy. This is what happened in the famous eruption of Vesuvius, which destroyed the town of Pompeii over 1900 years ago.

THE ERUPTION OF VESUVIUS, AD 79

At midday on 24th August, Vesuvius erupted, sending a cloud of ash, pumice and other rock 20 kilometres into the air. This covered Pompeii in 2 metres of rubble but it did not kill anyone.

After midnight, the cloud collapsed. It sent a surge of ash and hot gas mainly down the western slope of the mountain, at a speed of 160 kilometres per hour.

Early the next morning another surge of blistering ash and rock swept down the slopes. This time it covered the town of Pompeii and burnt and suffocated everyone there.

"Disaster Strikes"

As my uncle was leaving the house, he was handed a message from Rectina, whose house was at the foot of the mountain and whose escape was impossible except by boat. She was terrified of the danger threatening her and implored him to rescue her from her fate. He changed his plans, and what he had begun in a spirit of inquiry, he completed as a hero.

He gave orders for the ships to be launched and went on board himself with the intention of bringing help to many more people besides Rectina, for this lovely stretch of coast was thickly populated. He hurried to the place which everyone else was hastily leaving, steering his course straight for the danger zone. He was entirely fearless, describing each moment of the eruption to be noted down exactly as he observed it. Ashes were already falling, hotter and thicker as the ships drew near, followed by bits of pumice and blackened stones, charred and cracked by the flames.

Then, suddenly they were in shallow water, and the shore was blocked by the rubble from the mountain.

For a moment my uncle wondered whether to turn back, but when the helmsman advised this, my uncle refused, telling him that Fortune stood by the courageous …

Name _____   Class _____

PCM 6a (Levels 2–3)

Read 'Volcanoes' page 5, explain why volcanoes are dangerous, using words from the text to help you. First, complete the sentences with words from the text.

Paragraph 1
Lava is a mixture of _____ and _____
Volcanoes pour out streams of _____

Paragraph 2

Which word(s) tells us that volcanoes are very dangerous? _____

Using the words above and your own words explain why volcanoes are dangerous.

_____
_____
_____
_____
_____
_____
_____
_____
_____

PCM 6b (Levels 3–4)

Read Volcanoes page 5 and answer the question 'How are volcanoes dangerous?'

First, find and list any words/phrases that will help you.

Highlight/underline 3 words and use them in your answer.

_____
_____
_____
_____
_____
_____
_____

Name _____ Class _____

PCM 6c (Levels 4–5)

Levels 4–5

To answer the question 'How does the information in "Volcanoes" page 5 and "Disaster Strikes" page 7 show how dangerous volcanoes are?', make brief notes under the following headings. Then use words from the text to help you write a detailed answer.

What came out of the volcano? (Pages 5 and 7)

_____
_____
_____
_____
_____

What happened to Pompeii? (Page 5)

_____
_____
_____
_____
_____

How did people react? (Page 7)

_____
_____
_____
_____
_____

How does the information in "Volcanoes" page 5 and "Disaster Strikes" page 7 show how dangerous volcanoes are?

_____
_____
_____
_____
_____

Preparing for external tests is, of course, nothing new. Practising past paper questions (and answers!) and coaching of specific test techniques will certainly help your children prepare for the SATs. *But be careful that preparation does not 'take over' teaching and learning in your classroom!*

Preparing for *SATs*

The amount of SATs preparation you decide to do will depend on such things as: the ability of your children; past results; the attitudes of your Head, governors and other teaching staff; performance management and external pressures such as OFSTED, local authorities and parents. You need to strike a balance between two extremes.

Devoting most of the term before the SATs to test practice is too much. There will be a significant reduction in the time you spend on other curriculum areas and too narrow a concentration on test requirements in English. On the other hand, you will be only too aware that little or no preparation will disadvantage your children, and almost certainly affect your school's overall results.

Using past paper practice to teach test techniques will help your children handle the time constraints of the tests and give them greater confidence. You will find that their results invariably improve, practice paper by practice paper, as they understand what is expected of them and become more confident in tackling different types of question.

Working on one Reading Test paper every two to three weeks in the Spring Term will give your children sufficient practice. You can also select from the practical suggestions that follow in this section.

REMEMBER you need a balanced approach to test preparation in a subject like English, which is skills- rather than content-based. Good practice, **over the whole Key Stage**, is ideal.

PCM 7a SAT-NAV FOR TEACHERS

Do.......

- Create a positive climate:
  - build confidence with positive class, group and individual feedback
  - make the marker 'human' by introducing 'Sid and Sybil the SATs markers'; this makes the external marking process less threatening but also means that we can tell children what markers are looking for, to help them when they take the test
  - use a cartoon record sheet (see PCM 9, page 58)
  - use AfL approaches when working with test questions
  - see incorrect answers as learning opportunities
  - let children be 'markers'.

- Think about the content and interest level of the past papers you give children. Some of the most popular with children include 2007 – *On Dangerous Ground*, 2005 – *Travelling On*, 2004 – *You Can Do It*, 2003 – *To the Rescue* and 2000 – *Built to Last*. *Always* keep sets of past papers. Not only are they useful for test practice but they contain a number of varied and interesting texts which can be used in other lessons. Small extracts from past papers can be used to teach specific aspects of reading (see pages 53–55).

- Take the papers yourself. This will give you an insight into how children should tackle questions, plus some of the common pitfalls. It is especially important that once every two years or so, the whole staff (teachers and teaching assistants) takes the end-of-key-stage reading paper so that colleagues in Years 3, 4 and 5 understand what is expected of Year 6 children. It is particularly useful to do this with the reading test, as other papers can simply be displayed in the classroom for colleagues to examine. To take a whole reading test usually takes one staff meeting. Adults can be given less time than the children – seven minutes to read the text and 25 minutes to answer the questions. Papers do not have to be marked! Doing this will raise plenty of issues about the school's teaching of reading, and colleagues will gain valuable experience of the test requirements.

- Analyse both good and not-so-good responses. Model reading skills.

- Save the most recent test paper for the two weeks before the actual test.

- Teach specific test techniques as they arise in papers (see PCM 8, page 57, 'Sat-Nav for readers').

- Build in reflection time after tests have been marked. Help children to identify learning opportunities.

- Give careful thought as to whether to tell children scores and levels. This can be motivating or discouraging, depending on the child.

- Remember to set aside time for *reading for pleasure*. Sustained, silent reading time is never wasted, especially if, as a treat, children have a completely free choice of reading material.

PCM 7b

SAT-NAV for Year 6 teachers

Using past papers as a stimulus for literacy work in class

In the simple lesson ideas below, past test papers are used as a starting point for a range of reading and writing activities.

Resources:
2007 Reading Test Booklet: *On Dangerous Ground* (pages 9, 10 and 11), writing materials, highlighters (optional), holiday postcards (optional)

Simple lesson ideas

1 Spot the difference game

(Revising conventions of address lay-out)

Ask children to SPOT THE DIFFERENCE in the addresses below, circling any differences found. Discuss anomalies and write a correct version, individually or as a class.

MR A. Smith	Mr. A Smith,
No. 6, impala Drive	6 Impala drive
River Valley	river valley
Safariville.	safari ville,
UG12 3oh	UG12 30H

Consider the greetings and endings on postcards in the test booklet, (Dear All, Cheers, Neena and See you soon, Lisa). List appropriate alternatives.

2 Discuss the form, purpose and style of the picture postcard:

Picture postcards are:

- open (therefore general, not confidential information given)

- restricted (space is at a premium therefore sentences are often incomplete)

- sent to readers known to us (therefore the style is chatty, friendly, and personal openings/endings are used)

- meant to entertain and inform (therefore the writer selects details to inform the reader about events but also includes comments and opinions)

3 Sentence Level work

Taking an extract from each postcard – 'Mind you, I don't think the ruins will be here for ever' (Neena) and 'Had a great piece of luck' (Lisa), pick out subjects and verbs. Discuss the differences between the complete and incomplete sentence examples and the reasons why incomplete sentences are often found on postcards.

Ask children in pairs to read the postcards on page 9 of the 2007 Reading Test booklet, deciding whether sentences are complete or incomplete.

Which postcard has fewer incomplete sentences? What difference does this make?

4 Reading transformation

Using the advertisements on pages 10 and 11 of the 2007 Reading Test booklet (see also pages 77, 78 of this Handbook), children write a holiday postcard based on their visit to one of them.

Example 1 – based on Café Vesuvio – Naples

Dear Grandma and Grandad,
Am enjoying this great holiday in Italy. Yesterday we all went to a brilliant café in Naples – the Vesuvio. It was right near a boring museum which Mum dragged us round in the afternoon. Had the best pizza ever! Loads of scrummy tomatoes, peppers, mushrooms and sausage covered in tasty cheese. Yum! But there were also great veggie options, so Sally was happy (for once). You'd have loved it! The waiters were really friendly and we all stayed there eating and drinking until really late – eleven o'clock at night. Can you believe it? See you soon,
Love,
David

Postcards can be displayed with relevant art work or surrounding a model of a correctly written address.

Teaching complex inference – model lesson

AF3 – deduce, infer or interpret information, events or ideas from texts.

> Children find AF3 questions difficult. Using short extracts from test papers can help them make inferences sourced from the text, as in this 'Cool and Uncool Guesses' activity. The sequence below develops understanding through discussion rather than writing and helps children to discriminate between correct and incorrect inferences.

Imaginary teaching sequence based on Question 6 – Reading Paper 2006

Evelyn Glennie is a well-known musician who has played all round the world with famous orchestras. Here, Evelyn describes how she first became inspired to take up percussion instruments and how she 'hears' music even though she is deaf.

Once I went to secondary school I found there were many more percussion instruments to discover, which may be why I was so determined to try them.

I remember going through to the percussion room. It was tiny and what I saw was a xylophone, a couple of hand-tuned timpani, a drum kit, and an upright piano. I could hardly move. Mr Forbes, my teacher, told me to play some notes on the xylophone. He taught me how to develop my senses. He used to tell me to put my hands on the wall outside the music room and then he would play two notes on two drums and ask me, "Okay, which is the higher note?" I'd tell him which and he'd ask me how I knew. I'd tell him I could feel it maybe in the upper part of my hand. We'd discuss what was happening in my feet and legs as I played the drums, or listened to a piece of music.

Adapted from *Good Vibrations: my autobiography* by Evelyn Glennie

Mr Forbes taught Evelyn to develop her senses. For what other reasons is Mr Forbes important in Evelyn's life?

1 mark for each point to a max. of 2

The children will have one whiteboard between two and the 'guesses' will have been written on the board before the sequence.

Teacher: What does the question ask us to do?
Child 1: Say why Mr Forbes is important in Evelyn's life.
Teacher: Is there another part of the question with a key word in it – a word that we should underline perhaps?
Child 2: It says 'other reasons'.
Teacher: What do you now think the question wants us to do?
Child 3: We're told he taught her to develop her senses, so if it says 'other reasons' it means we need to say something else different from that.
Teacher: Well spotted. Now who can find a sentence in which Evelyn mentions Mr Forbes and read it out for us?
Child 4: Mr Forbes, my teacher, told me to play some notes on the xylophone. He taught me how to develop my senses.

Teacher underlines sentences.

Teacher: Can anyone else find a sentence which mentioned what else Mr Forbes did that might be important to Evelyn?
Child 5: We'd discuss what was happening in my feet and legs.

Teacher underlines sentence.

Teacher: We have quite a problem here. The writing does not actually tell us why Mr Forbes is important in Evelyn's life. We are going to have to do some guessing but as you know it has got to be guessing based on the writing and the answer must be more than simply 'copied out' from the writing.

*The children now spend 5 minutes looking at the guesses. On their whiteboards they write the number of the question and next to it CG (Cool Guess) or UG (Uncool Guess) or any other code of the teacher's choice.
In pairs, they have to discuss how they know which is which and they may highlight parts of the text to help with identification.*

Guesses:

1 *Mr Forbes was her PE teacher.* (UG – although the writing mentions feet and legs it says my teacher told me to play some notes on the xylophone. It also says the percussion room not the gym or hall.)

2 *Mr Forbes helped her so she could play percussion.* (CG – because the writing says told me to play some notes.)

3 *Mr Forbes only taught Evelyn once and then gave up because she was deaf.* (UG – because the writing says 'he used to' and 'I'd tell him' and 'We'd discuss' so I think this means it happened more than once.

4 *Mr Forbes introduced her to a lot more percussion instruments.* (CG – the writing says at secondary school there were many more percussion instruments to discover.)

5 *Mr Forbes believed that Evelyn could play music.* (CG – As guess No. 3 because he didn't give up. He kept helping her.)

The sequence closes with a brief discussion of the 'guesses' and the supporting evidence in the text.

Preparing for SATs

Photocopy masters – notes for teachers

The following notes explain how to use the Photocopy Masters on pages 57 to 74.

PCM 8
SAT-NAV for readers (page 57): Use this sheet to remind children of important aspects to bear in mind when they are sitting externally-marked tests.

PCM 9
My reading test record (page 58): Year 6 children use this sheet to record their own marks from each practice past paper.

PCM 10
Giving an opinion (pages 59–60): This activity relates to AF6 and demonstrates how to use a past paper extract to explain the appeal of a text. Children analyse example answers and then write their own explanation.

PCMs 11–13
Reading 'Solos' – I can write interesting questions: A favourite fact book and I know how a fact book is organised (pages 61–63): The aim of the Reading 'Solo' Photocopy Masters is to encourage independence. Once the use of these sheets has been modelled, children can use them whenever wished.

PCM 14
I can work out meanings of words I do not know (page 64): This gives practice in using context and other clues to help work out unknown words.

PCM 15
I can work out words or phrases with more than one meaning (page 64): These sheets practise explaining words and phrases with more than one meaning, using jokes. Children make a collection of their own examples.

PCM 16
Text features: What job does it do? (page 66): A short quiz to test children's knowledge of text features. Note that, sometimes, more than one definition can be ticked!

PCMs 17–18
Special kinds of writing (pages 67–68): Separate PCMS for Lower and Upper KS2 encourage children to ask the questions they need to determine the purpose of texts (AF6).

PCM 19
WANTED (page 69): Children fill in an advert for a specific text feature (AF4) by considering what the feature does and what it needs to be to carry out its job in a particular text. They collect examples independently. The example given focuses on subheadings, but similar sheets could also be created for other text features.

PCM 20
Fiction brainteasers (page 70): An assessment sheet which also provides teachers with a checklist of key questions to ask children during one-to-one discussions about poetry or fiction. The sheet includes questions relevant to both fiction and poetry, and can be used with any story or poem. Using the criteria for each Assessment Focus on pages 12–18, teachers can make a simple judgement about the level of a child's response.

PCMs 21–22
Guided reading records (pages 71–72): These PCMs can be used to record group and individual responses during guided reading sessions and also assist with planning work to be covered.

PCM 23
Reading and responding to poetry (page 73) is a self-assessment sheet giving grouped criteria for children to record their skills when reading poetry, and also provides targets for further improvement.

PCM 24
My literacy buddy agreement (page 74) provides children with a set of rules for working with a 'Buddy' in Literacy. It should be given to and discussed with children so that they are aware of the important issues and ground rules for working with and giving feedback to other children.

Name _____ Class _____

PCM 8

SAT-NAV for readers

Get into gear to find your way round the reading paper!

Before you move off …

- use the full 15 minutes reading time. If you have time left over, go back to a text which you found slightly more difficult and read it again.
- use a finger to read. This helps your eyes and brain 'chunk' the text so that you understand it better.
- think about the WHOLE booklet. Which text did you like best and why? Why has the booklet been given its title? How are the texts the same or different?

During the test …

- ALWAYS look back to the text. Don't rely on memory. TEXT IT!
- read questions carefully right to the end.
- underline KEY WORDS in the questions.
- do as the question says. If it asks for TWO, only give two. If it asks you to look at page 10, make sure you answer from that page.
- do not write out the question again.
- begin answers with 'because' or 'so' if that is quicker.
- use bullet points for longer answers if appropriate.

- match answers to marks available. Listen carefully to your teacher's instructions.
- for 3 mark answers remember to P.E.E. where appropriate (make a Point, use Evidence and give an Explanation).
- do not spend too long on questions you find difficult. In the last five minutes, look ahead to see if there are easier questions you might still answer.
- if you have time left, add more to your 3 mark answers.
- make sure your handwriting can be read but don't spend too long making it your neatest handwriting.

Name _____ Class _____

PCM 9

Name _____ Class _____

My reading test record

Use this record sheet to record your marks on each past paper.

SATsuma

SATellite

SATurate

Date	Name of paper	Mark received

Name _____ Class _____

PCM 10

Giving an opinion

When asked to give your opinion on a text, think about what the text says (**content**) and **how** it says it or **how** the writer uses words (**style**).

Hadrian's Wall

When you get there, you'll probably wonder why you ever bothered to trudge up to this desolate part of Britain. Bits of the wall are crumbling and no taller than a molehill. The stones are now under attack from moss and sheep rather than savage Celtic tribes. But instead of moaning, just close your eyes and imagine the wall as it was in the year 130 AD, newly built, 5 metres high and stretching 120 kilometres across the country. Roman soldiers were stationed there to protect the Empire from attack.

Picture this: hordes of terrifying spiky-haired Celt warriors, their bodies painted blue, whirling their swords above their heads and screaming battlecries. No wonder the Romans wanted to keep them out!

In these answers, children explain why they like the writing about Hadrian's Wall.

Jane: *I enjoyed Hadrian's Wall best because it tells you in a funny way.*

Jack: *Hadrian's Wall is best because it mentions some funny things in it.*

Amir: *Hadrian's Wall because it's amusing when the last sentences say 'Romans wanted to keep out' and 'spiky-haired Celtic warriors'.*

Tracy: *I enjoyed Hadrian's Wall most. The writer helps you to imagine you were there with phrases like 'Picture this'. He describes the Celts well using interesting words 'bodies painted blue whirling their swords'. He uses lots of detail, e.g. '130 AD, newly built' which gives facts but also describes it in an amusing way.*

(Continued on next page)

Name _____ Class _____

PCM 10
Giving an opinion (continued . . .)

What does each answer include about the facts in the writing?

Has the answer included 'quotes'?

What does the answer say about **how** it is written?

Review the answers below.

Jane only _____
_____
_____
_____

Jack has _____
_____
_____
_____

Amir mentions _____
_____
_____
_____

Tracy _____
_____
_____
_____

Now give your own opinion. What do you **like** or **dislike** about the writing?
_____
_____
_____
_____
_____

Name _____ Class _____

PCM 11

Reading 'Solos': I can write interesting questions

Below are some reading 'Solos' to help you think of questions independently.

Use them to write THREE different questions about the text for your reading partner to answer. Choose ONE from each section.

Fact 'Solos'	Who	?
	When	?
	Why	?
	Where	?
	What	?
	How	?

Opinion 'Solos'	Why do you think	?
	Did you like	?
	Why or why not	?
	Which is your favourite	?
	Why	?
	How did you feel when	?
	Why	?
	Is the writing true to life	?
	Explain.	

Prediction 'Solos'	What might happen	?
	Where will	?
	How will	?

Name _____   Class _____

PCM 12

Reading 'Solos': A favourite factual book

Before you start the book

Look at the COVER and the 'BLURB' on the back

- What does it **show** the reader? _____
  _____

- In your own words what does it **tell** the reader? _____
  _____
  _____

Turn to the CONTENTS page

- Choose **three** of the sections in the contents
  _____   _____   _____

- Write **two** questions about things you would like to know for each section
  _____
  _____

Turn to the INDEX

- Choose **one** item from the index _____
- Write **two** interesting questions about it _____
  _____

Read the book

1 What is the most interesting thing in the book?
2 What have you found most useful in the book?
3 What has surprised you in this book?
4 Find **two** examples of where the writer gives an opinion. What do they think?
5 Choose one picture. Explain what the picture shows and what it helps the reader to understand.
6 Look at a double page. How is the reader helped to find information?
7 Either discuss or write answers to the questions you wrote down before you read the book.

Name _____ Class _____

PCM 13

Reading 'Solos': I know how a factual book is organised

Give the page number to show where we can find: *Contents* _____ *Index* _____	Different types of illustration	*A drawing* page _____
Give one example of: *A main heading:* page _____	Describe what each shows and give the page number *A photograph* page _____	List 5 NEW WORDS that this book has given you. Give the meaning of each word. **1** **2**
A sub-heading: page _____	*A diagram* 	**3** **4**
A caption page _____	page _____	**5**

For this topic, how good a book do you think it is? Explain your answer.

Name _____   Class _____

PCM 14

I can work out meanings of words I do not know

For these questions you are asked to say what a word or phrase means. Unfortunately, you cannot use a thesaurus or dictionary. If you do not understand the word or phrase, reading the rest of the sentence might help you to work it out. With a partner, try to work out the meaning of the underlined words and **then** check in the dictionary.

a When Sam made a mistake in his book, he took a rubber and tried to <u>erase</u> it.

Guess _____

Because _____

Dictionary definition _____

b "Your teacher says that you often disturb the others on your table. You are too <u>loquacious</u>!"

Guess _____

Because _____

Dictionary definition _____

c Because he believed he was innocent, the man tried to <u>rebut</u> the charge.

Guess _____

Because _____

Dictionary definition _____

d After an amazing night out, Sarah was sorry that the gig was over, but she cheered herself up by looking at a <u>memento</u> of the concert.

Guess _____

Because _____

Dictionary definition _____

e To <u>staunch</u> the blood that was flowing from the wound, the First Aider put a bandage over it and pressed down.

Guess _____

Because _____

Dictionary definition _____

Name _____ Class _____

PCM 15

I can work out words or phrases with more than one meaning

Often writers use words with more than one meaning when they are trying to entertain the reader or make them think. Jokes often have words or phrases with more than one meaning.

Doctor, doctor I've got jelly in one ear and custard in the other. What's wrong with me? Don't worry! You're just a <u>trifle</u> deaf!

The word 'trifle' has more than one meaning. It can mean 'little' or it can mean 'a pudding made with jelly and custard.'

Try reading the jokes below with a friend. Underline the words with more than one meaning. Then explain the two meanings.

a *Why did the pilot crash into the house?*
Because they left the landing light on.

Meaning 1 _____

Meaning 2 _____

b *Why did the cat help out at the hospital?*
Because it wanted to be a first-aid kit.

Meaning 1 _____

Meaning 2 _____

c *Did you hear about the thieves who stole a large hole?*
Police are looking into it.

Meaning 1 _____

Meaning 2 _____

Use a joke book to find some favourite jokes with words that have two meanings. Write them out and underline the word or phrase with two meanings. Draw a picture for each joke.

Name _____   Class _____

PCM 16

Text features: What job does it do?

Try the quiz below.
In each box there is a statement.
Tick ALL the statements that you think are true.

> **TOP TIPS**
> Look at a number of different books in the school library.
> Can you find examples of each feature below?

1 Sub-headings			
tell us what the chapter is about ☐	tell us what the next paragraph is about ☐	tell us what the pictures are about ☐	tell us what the page is about ☐

2 A glossary			
is the 'blurb' on the back cover ☐	tells us where we can find words ☐	explains what a word means ☐	separates a part of the text ☐

3 Brackets ( )			
give extra information ☐	show us which way round to read a text ☐	separate pieces of text ☐	explain abbreviations e.g. (HGV) ☐

4 A main heading			
tells us what the next paragraph is about ☐	tells us what the picture is about ☐	introduces the whole text ☐	

5 A picture in a story			
helps us to imagine what things in the story look like ☐	tells us the story ☐	shows us what is happening ☐	

6 An index			
tells you where to find something in a book ☐	tells you what the whole chapter is about ☐	tells you the meanings of words ☐	

7 A diagram is			
something that separates writing ☐	a plan of something ☐	a line drawing which helps the reader picture what the writing is talking about ☐	

8 An ellipsis …			
shows that time has passed	can show a moment of tension	is a decoration	

9 A caption			
tells us more about a picture	is a kind of heading	introduces a paragraph	

10 A table of information			
tells us the contents	separates information	sorts information	

11 A contents page			
explains unknown words	lists words alphabetically	tells us what is in the book	

Name _____   Class _____

PCM 17 Special kinds of writing – Lower KS2

I can work out the type of text I am reading and can say why it has been written and who the audience is.

There are many different kinds of writing. It all depends on WHAT you're writing about, WHY you are writing and WHO you are writing for.

Read the pieces of writing below and work out WHAT, WHY and WHO for each piece. Also think about what the writing would need to have to make it a good one of its type.

What kind of writing is it?
diary? newspaper report? story? factual? set of instructions? letter? information leaflet? playscript?

Why has it been written?
Is it to: explain? introduce? summarise? give information? persuade? instruct? entertain? inspire? describe?

Who is the audience?
younger people? older people? teachers? children? sports people? musicians? etc.

Example

Beat the eggs. Gradually stir them into the flour. Add raisins or chocolate chips. Blend well. Put into a cake tin. Bake in the oven at 180°.	What: recipe Why: to tell you how to make a cake Who: someone cooking

1	So, the three little pigs walked off hand in hand feeling very pleased that they had managed to defeat the wolf.	What: Why: Who:
2	What a disaster! Forgot my lunchbox. Slipped on the dining room floor and hurt my ankle. Remind me not to get up tomorrow!	What: Why: Who:
3	Will he like it? He'll love it! The dog hasn't been born that doesn't like Doggydates – the delicacy all dogs will die for!	What: Why: Who:
4	It rose, silently but menacingly. Leaving the Black Lagoon, it made its deadly way towards the sleeping town.	What: Why: Who:

Name _____ Class _____

PCM 18 Special kinds of writing – Upper KS2

I can work out the type of text I am reading and can say why it has been written and who the audience is.

There are many different kinds of writing. It all depends on WHAT you're writing about, WHY you are writing and WHO you are writing for. Read the pieces of writing below and work out WHAT, WHY and WHO for each piece. Also think about what the writing would need to have to make it a good one of its type.

What kind of writing is it?
diary? newspaper report? story? factual? set of instructions? letter? information leaflet? playscript?

Why has it been written?
Is it to: explain? introduce? summarise? give information? persuade? instruct? entertain? inspire? describe?

Who is the audience?
younger people? older people? teachers? children? sports people? musicians? etc.

1	I am sorry to have to inform you that unless your daughter begins to behave in the way the school expects all its pupils to behave, we will be asking you to attend an interview to discuss her future.	What: Why: Who:
2	John Smith was never an average player. By the age of eleven he was playing in an adult side and scoring goals regularly against tough opposition.	What: Why: Who:
3	We regret that we are unable to forward the goods you requested because we are out of stock at the moment. However, we shall contact you again as soon as the position changes.	What: Why: Who:
4	Unless we act now to recycle everything we can, landfill sites will shortly become full and we will have nowhere to deposit our rubbish.	What: Why: Who:
5	On the other hand, many children would disagree with this view. They would like to be able to wear their own clothes to school instead of a uniform.	What: Why: Who:
6	As well as the Olympics, the Ancient Greeks have also given us a style of architecture.	What: Why: Who:

Name _____   Class _____

PCM 19

WANTED

A text feature whose job is to tell us what the next paragraph is going to be about.

Must be: **Clear**   **Bold**   **Informative**   **Accurate**

Only _____ with at least three years experience should apply.

Now collect some examples of the feature above and write or stick them in the space below.

Name _____ Class _____

PCM 20

Fiction brainteasers

Question	AFs	Level			
		2	3	4	5
1 What happens in the story?	2				
2 What is the most exciting part of the story and why?	2 & 3				
3 How do the characters feel at this point?	3				
4 What changes after this point in the story?	2 & 3				
5 Where and when is the story set? Does the setting make a difference?	2 & 7				
6 Who is your favourite/least favourite character? Why?	2, 3 & 6				
7 Name two less important characters. What part do they play in the story?	3 & 6				
8 Which other stories/poems have you read by this writer? Which is your favourite and why?	6 & 7				
9 Which phrases or lines in the poem are your favourite? Explain why.	5 & 6				
10 If you were asked to give this poem a different title and last line what would you choose and why?	2, 3 & 6				

PCM 21

Guided reading record 1

Date _____ Group Name _____ Text _____

Question	Child	Response	AF
1			
2			
3			
4			
5			
6			

PCM 22
Guided reading record 2

Date _____ Group name _____ Text _____

Text task _____

Children: 1 _____ 2 _____ 3 _____

4 _____ 5 _____ 6 _____ 7 _____

Questions	AF	Child's initials	Response		
			Tick	Cross	Partly

Name _____ Class _____

PCM 23

Reading and responding to poetry

Poem _____ By _____

Tick the statement in each group of three below which best describes what you can do.

- [ ] I can look back at the poem when explaining what it is about.
- [ ] I can find and quote the poet's words to support answers.
- [ ] I can find and quote KEY words/phrases to support answers.

- [ ] I can explain what happens in a poem.
- [ ] I can work out the order of ideas in a poem and identify an obvious theme.
- [ ] I can identify ways in which poets present issues and summarise themes.

- [ ] I can begin to understand why writers use particular words (e.g. to make us laugh) and pick out examples of effective language.
- [ ] I can recognise language features and explain in simple terms their effect on the reader.
- [ ] I can understand how words affect a reader's thoughts/feelings, identify key words/phrases and explain their effect.

- [ ] I can pick out one or two obvious things that are the same or different in two poems.
- [ ] I can pick out details that are the same or different in two or more poems.
- [ ] I can begin to analyse similarities and differences in two or more poems, with detailed explanations.

- [ ] I can express simply what I like or dislike.
- [ ] I can express personal response with one example of supporting detail.
- [ ] I can develop a justified personal response to one or more poems.

Name _____   Class _____

PCM 24

My literacy buddy agreement

To be really good 'buddies' we need to agree some basic rules.

1 We value the work our 'buddy' is showing us. We only discuss it with them.

2 We give it our full attention and read it carefully.

3 We listen carefully to each other when we talk about our work and the targets we have tried to meet.

4 We understand that effort has gone into our work and praise each other when we have tried hard.

5 We pick out the things our 'buddy' has done well.

6 We concentrate mainly on the lesson learning targets.

7 When helping each other, we think about 'small step' improvements.

8 We need to listen carefully to what our buddy or our teacher tells us about our work and then think about it. Then we will make most progress.

Date _____

Signed _____

Signed _____

Glossary of terms

APP – Assessing Pupil Progress: an assessment approach developed by QCA and the National Strategies. It gives teachers a profile of a child's strengths and weaknesses using evidence from ongoing classroom work. Based on a considered judgement of a child's attainment in all seven Reading **Assessment Focuses**, it also provides teachers with a national curriculum level if required. Judgements are based on evidence from a wide range of contexts and curriculum areas.

Assessment Focuses: seven broad areas which form the focus for children's work and teachers' assessments in Reading. Each Assessment Focus covers a separate aspect of children's reading (see below). Criteria for each Assessment Focus are used by teachers to determine a National Curriculum level for children's work, e.g. as part of **APP**.
AF1 – using a range of strategies to decode and access texts
AF2 – understanding of, describing, selecting or retrieving information, events or ideas from texts using quotation and textual references
AF3 – deducing, inferring or interpreting information, events or ideas
AF4 – identifying and commenting on the structure and organisation of texts
AF5 – explaining and commenting on writers' use of language
AF6 – identifying and commenting on writers' purposes and viewpoints and the overall effect of the text on the reader
AF7 – relating texts to their social, cultural and historical contexts and literary traditions.

Assessment for learning: which might be seen as 'day-to-day' assessment, is a process which is concerned not just with outcomes, but with promoting the whole learning process. By establishing a classroom climate in which both teachers and learners are actively engaged in this process, assessment has more impact and value.

Authorial intent: recognition of a writer's purpose or the effect a writer is trying to achieve.

Criteria: principles used as standards in judging children's attainment.

EKSAs: End of Key Stage Assessments, also commonly known as SATs.

External marking: marking, usually of test materials, carried out by a recognised authority outside school. Currently **EKSAs**, some QCA optional tests and single level tests are marked externally.

Formative assessment: is the process by which a teacher observes, evaluates, discusses or marks a piece of work and identifies specific strengths and weaknesses in it in order to provide a focus for teacher/student discussion and student self-analysis/reflection.

Level descriptors: general statements describing typical attainment at each National Curriculum level in Speaking and Listening, Reading and Writing (see Primary Framework).

Level discriminators: criteria used by examiners, which mark the main differences between one National Curriculum level and the next.

Metacognition: self-awareness related to learning and central to children's participation in assessment for learning; e.g. when a child reflects on what and how they have learnt, and what they need to do next to learn more.

Single Level tests: tests of reading at one national curriculum level developed from national curriculum descriptors and **APP** criteria. Used to substantiate teacher judgements as to whether a child is working securely at a particular level.

Summative assessment: is the feedback given to a student at the end of a marked piece of work which highlights strengths and weaknesses to be addressed. It is also a term which can be used to describe more formal end-of-unit or end-of-phase tests.

Assessment game:
A DAY IN POMPEII

(Based on texts from pages 10, 11 in the 2007 Reading Test Paper 'On Dangerous Ground')

Inside the back cover of this book you will find a fold-out game board.

You will need:

▶ Fold-out game

▶ 1 dice

▶ 1 counter per player

▶ Copy of texts from pages 10, 11 of 2007 Reading Test Paper (see pages 77, 78).

This non-competitive game is designed so that children answer questions on Reading Assessment Focuses 2 – 6. The aim is not to be the first to finish but for the children to answer questions on all Assessment Focuses as well as they can, using the text to support them. Players take turns to roll the dice and move their counters the appropriate number of squares forward. Whichever square (a – e) children land on, they then answer the corresponding question for that Assessment Focus. Answers may be oral or written down. Children can play as individuals, but should discuss answers with fellow players. The analysis of text which takes place when reading 'buddies' discuss answers can be very valuable.

A Day in Pompeii

Visit Vesuvius by Rail

Don't miss this unique journey, only a short trip from Pompeii itself!

* Travel by mountain railway to the very summit *
* Peer into the enormous crater *
* See the volcano in action *
* Departures every hour from Pompeii town square *

P.S. Don't forget your camera!

Not sure where to go?
Not sure what to see?
Why not try Lucio's all-inclusive guided walking tour?

We'll show you the best of Pompeii

Highlights include:

Museum visit • The house of the silver wedding
The central baths • Designing your own mosaic
Dressing up in a toga • Activities for children

GOOD VALUE

• discounts for students, senior citizens, children and families!

Departs:

Main Gate, 10am and 2pm

Bay of Naples Museum

Mount Vesuvius is the world's most studied volcano! Here at the Bay of Naples Museum, we have combined information about the formation of volcanoes with objects of interest from Pompeii and the surrounding area. Our detailed exhibits show the layers of rock within the mountain, and a small-scale replica of the town of Pompeii.

... bringing the past back to life

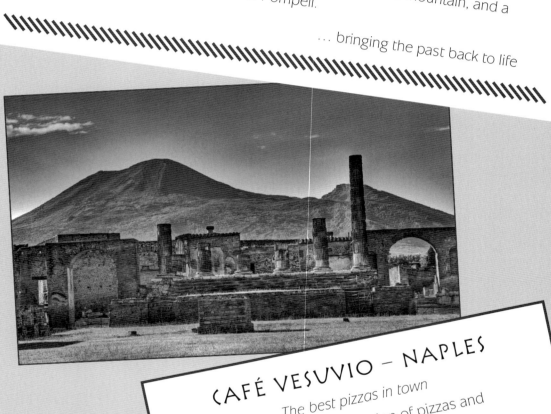

CAFÉ VESUVIO – NAPLES

The best pizzas in town

We offer a wide selection of pizzas and pasta meals at modest prices.

Vegetarian dishes available.

Family business – friendly atmosphere.

Open 11am to 11pm

Round the corner from the museum!

Assessment game: A DAY IN POMPEII

Answers for 'A Day in Pompeii' board game

AF2 True or false?

a False. It also serves 'pasta meals'.

b True. The exhibits show us what the layers of rocks inside the mountain look like.

c True. It goes to the 'very summit'.

d False. We are only told the time the tour departs.

e True. The café is only 'round the corner' from the Museum.

AF3

a They suggest that the atmosphere in the café is welcoming ('friendly'), that their food is very good ('best pizzas') and that there is a big choice ('wide selection') which would help you to enjoy eating there.

b 'In action'

c A guide takes you and it mentions that it is suitable for children and senior citizens. You get to do lots of other interesting things like dressing up and art so it is not just for experienced walkers.

d 'short trip' (Visit Vesuvius by Rail)

e It shows a real house from the past so you know how they lived. You also have the chance to dress up in the clothes the people of Pompeii wore as well as designing a mosaic.

AF4

a Sentences 1 and 2 use the exclamation marks in different ways. In 1) it is encouraging you to eat there by telling you a list of brilliant things about the café. In sentence 2 it is acting as a reminder or warning not to forget your camera.

b It is the main heading which tells you what the whole text is about. It needs to stand out clearly and give the information as a brief title.

c The photographs help you to see what some of the places described in the text are like. They might also encourage you to visit these places.

d The ellipsis is introducing the Museum's slogan.

e This is a personal choice. Think about headings, bullet points, highlighted text, layout of sections etc.

AF5

a 'replica'

b That the journey is special. There is no other journey like it.

c The writer uses words like 'world's most studied volcano' to make you think the volcano is very interesting. He tells us that we will see 'objects of interest' and will get to know what it was like then, 'bringing the past back to life'.

d Well-chosen words like 'peer', 'enormous crater' and 'unique journey' make the visit sound special. You are also told to remember your camera so it must be exciting.

e Personal opinion. Think about words used and the way they are used. Is it persuasive if questions are asked? Does the P.S. persuade you because it is like a real person talking to you?

AF6

a Choose between Lucio's tour and Café Vesuvio. Look at what the adverts say that would make the visit good for families.

b If you are tourists you might not know what to do or see. He is trying to suggest that the answer lies on his tour and you should go with him.

c It makes you think someone is speaking to you and advising you.

d He is trying to separate the things that you can do but also make the advert clearer and more appealing by highlighting the important things like value for money, time it leaves and activities.

e Personal opinion. Remember to use words from the text to explain your choice.

Acknowledgements

The author and publisher would like to thank the following for permission to reproduce material:

Les Baynton

Qualifications and Curriculum Authority (QCA Enterprises Ltd)

Photographs:

© BananaStock Ltd, except p77 © Brian Harris / Alamy, p78 © Stewart Wallace / Alamy